DATE DUE

Creation of the Modern Middle East

Turkey

Creation of the Modern Middle East

Turkey

Heather Lehr Wagner

Introduction by
Akbar Ahmed
School of International Service
American University

CHELSEA HOUSE
PUBLISHERS
A Haights Cross Communications Company
Philadelphia

Frontispiece: Turkish Man
An undated photograph of a Turk with pistols and bared sword. The Turks' warlike reputation goes back to the time of their ancestors.

CHELSEA HOUSE PUBLISHERS

EDITOR IN CHIEF Sally Cheney
DIRECTOR OF PRODUCTION Kim Shinners
CREATIVE MANAGER Takeshi Takahashi
MANUFACTURING MANAGER Diann Grasse

Staff for TURKEY

EDITOR Lee Marcott
PRODUCTION ASSISTANT Jaimie Winkler
PICTURE RESEARCHER Sarah Bloom
SERIES AND COVER DESIGNER Keith Trego
LAYOUT 21st Century Publishing and Communications, Inc.

A Haights Cross Communications ✦ Company

http://www.chelseahouse.com

First Printing

1 3 5 7 9 8 6 4 2

Library of Congress Cataloging-in-Publication Data

Wagner, Heather Lehr.
    Turkey / by Heather Lehr Wagner.
        p. cm. — (Creation of the modern Middle East)
Includes bibliographical references and index.
    ISBN 0-7910-6504-9
    1. Turkey—History—20th century. I. Title. II. Series.
DR576 .W34 2002
956.1'02—dc21
                                                    2002001401

Table of Contents

Index to the Photographs

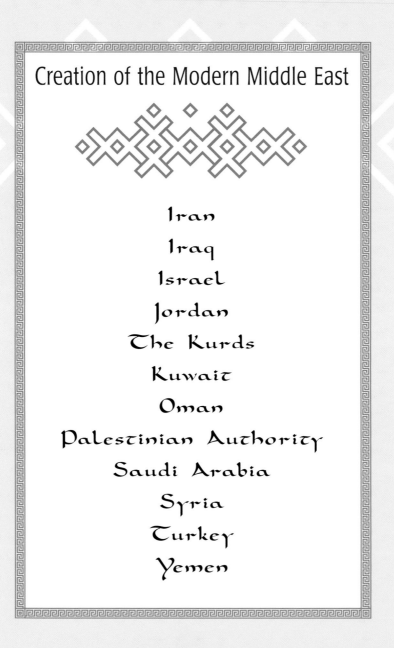

Creation of the Modern Middle East

Iran

Iraq

Israel

Jordan

The Kurds

Kuwait

Oman

Palestinian Authority

Saudi Arabia

Syria

Turkey

Yemen

Introduction

The Middle East, it seems, is always in the news. Unfortunately, most of the news is of a troubling kind. Stories of suicide bombers, hijackers, street demonstrations, and ongoing violent conflict dominate these reports. The conflict draws in people living in lands far from the Middle East; some support one group, some support another, often on the basis of kinship or affinity and not on the merits of the case.

The Middle East is often identified with the Arabs. The region is seen as peopled by Arabs speaking Arabic and belonging to the Islamic faith. The stereotype of the Arab oil sheikh is a part of contemporary culture. But both of these images—that the Middle East is in perpetual anarchy and that it has an exclusive Arab identity—are oversimplifications of the region's complex contemporary reality.

In reality, the Middle East is an area that straddles Africa and Asia and has a combined population of over 200 million people inhabiting over twenty countries. It is a region that draws the entire world into its politics and, above all, it is the land that is the birth place of the three great Abrahamic faiths—Judaism, Christianity, and Islam. The city of Jerusalem is the point at which these three faiths come together and also where they tragically confront one another.

It is for these reasons that knowledge of the Middle East will remain of importance and that news from it will remain ongoing and interesting.

Let us consider the stereotype of the Middle East as a land of constant anarchy. It is easy to forget that some of the greatest lawgivers and people of peace were born, lived, and died here. In the Abrahamic tradition these names are a glorious roll call of human history—Abraham, Moses, Jesus, and Muhammad. In the tradition of the Middle East, where these names are especially revered, people often add the blessing "Peace be upon him" when speaking their names.

The land is clearly one that is shared by the great faiths. While it has a dominant Muslim character because of the large Muslim population, its Jewish and Christian presence must not be underestimated. Indeed, it is the dynamics of the relationships between the three faiths that allow us to enter the Middle East today and appreciate the points where these faiths come together or are in conflict.

To understand the predicament in which the people of the Middle East find themselves today, it is well to keep the facts of history before us. History is never far from the minds of the people in this region. Memories of the first great Arab dynasty, the Umayyads (661-750), based in Damascus, and the even greater one of the Abbasids (750-1258), based in Baghdad, are still kept alive in books and folklore. For the Arabs, their history, their culture, their tradition, their language, and above all their religion, provide them with a rich source of pride; but the glory of the past contrasts with the reality and powerlessness of contemporary life.

Many Arabs have blamed past rulers for their current situation beginning with the Ottomans who ruled them until World War I and then the European powers that divided their lands. When they achieved independence after World War II they discovered that the artificial boundaries created by the European powers cut across tribes and clans. Today, too, they complain that a form of Western imperialism still dominates their politics and rulers.

Again, while it is true that Arab history and Arab temperament have colored the Middle East strongly, there are other distinct peoples who have made a significant contribution to the culture of the region. Turkey is one such non-Arab nation with its own language, culture, and contribution to the region through the influence of the Ottoman Empire. Memories of that period for the Arabs are mixed, but what cannot be denied are the spectacular administrative and architectural achievements of the Ottomans. It is the longest dynasty in world history, beginning in 1300 and ending after World War I in 1922, when Kemal Ataturk wished to reject the past on the way to creating a modern Turkey.

Similarly, Iran is another non-Arab country with its own rich language and culture. Based in the minority sect of Islam, the Shia, Iran has often been in opposition to its Sunni neighbors, both Arab and Turk. Perhaps this confrontation helped to forge a unique Iranian, or Persian, cultural identity that, in turn, created the brilliant art, architecture, and poetry under the Safawids (1501-1722). The Safawid period also saw the establishment of the principle of interference or participation—depending on one's perspective—in matters of the state by the religious clerics. So while the Ayatollah Khomeini was very much a late 20th century figure, he was nonetheless reflecting the patterns of Iranian history.

Israel, too, represents an ancient, non-Arabic, cultural and religious tradition. Indeed, its very name is linked to the tribes that figure prominently in the stories of the Bible and it is through Jewish tradition that memory of the great biblical patriarchs like Abraham and Moses is kept alive. History is not a matter of years, but of millennia, in the Middle East.

Perhaps nothing has evoked as much emotional and political controversy among the Arabs as the creation of the state of Israel in 1948. With it came ideas of democracy and modern culture that seemed alien to many Arabs. Many saw the wars that followed stir further conflict and hatred; they also saw the wars as an inevitable clash between Islam and Judaism.

It is therefore important to make a comment on Islam and Judaism. The roots of prejudice against Jews can be anti-Semitic, anti-Judaic, and anti-Zionist. The prejudice may combine all three and there is often a degree of overlap. But in the case of the Arabs, the matter is more complicated because, by definition, Arabs cannot be anti-Semitic because they themselves are considered Semites. They cannot be anti-Judaic, because Islam recognizes the Jews as "people of the Book."

What this leaves us with is the clash between the political philosophy of Zionism, which is the establishment of a Jewish nation in Palestine, and Arab thought. The antagonism of the Arabs to Israel may result in the blurring of lines. A way must be found by Arabs and Israelis to live side by side in peace. Perhaps recognition of the common Abrahamic tradition is one way forward.

The hostility to Israel partly explains the negative coverage the Arabs get in the Western media. Arab Muslims are often accused of being anarchic and barbaric due to the violence of the Middle East. Yet, their history has produced some of the greatest figures in history.

Consider the example of Sultan Salahuddin Ayyoubi, popularly called Saladin in Western literature. Saladin had vowed to take revenge for the bloody massacres that the Crusaders had indulged in when they took Jerusalem in 1099. According to a European eyewitness account the blood in the streets was so deep that it came up to the knees of the horsemen.

Yet, when Saladin took Jerusalem in 1187, he showed the essential compassion and tolerance that is at the heart of the Abrahamic faiths. He not only released the prisoners after ransom, as was the custom, but paid for those who were too poor to afford any ransom. His nobles and commanders were furious that he had not taken a bloody revenge. Saladin is still remembered in the bazaars and villages as a leader of great learning and compassion. When contemporary leaders are compared to Saladin, they are usually found wanting. One reason may be that the problems of the region are daunting.

The Middle East faces three major problems that will need solutions in the twenty-first century. These problems affect society and politics and need to be tackled by the rulers in those lands and all other people interested in creating a degree of dialogue and participation.

The first of the problems is that of democracy. Although democracy is practiced in some form in a number of the Arab countries, for the majority of ordinary people there is little sense of participation in their government. The frustration of helplessness in the face of an indifferent bureaucracy at the lower levels of administration is easily converted to violence. The indifference of the state to the pressing needs of the "street" means that other non-governmental organizations can step in. Islamic organizations offering health and education programs to people in the shantytowns and villages have therefore emerged and flourished over the last decades.

The lack of democracy also means that the ruler becomes remote and autocratic over time as he consolidates his power. It is not uncommon for many rulers in the Middle East to pass on their rule to their son. Dynastic rule, whether kingly or based in a dictatorship, excludes ordinary people from a sense of participation in their own governance. They need to feel empowered. Muslims need to feel that they are able to participate in the process of government. They must feel that they are able to elect their leaders into office and if these leaders do not deliver on their promises, that they can throw them out. Too many of the rulers are nasty and brutish. Too many Muslim leaders are kings and military dictators. Many of them ensure that their sons or relatives stay on to perpetuate their dynastic rule.

With democracy, Muslim peoples will be able to better bridge the gaps that are widening between the rich and the poor. The sight of palatial mansions with security guards carrying automatic weapons standing outside them and, alongside, hovels teeming with starkly poor children is a common one in Muslim cities. The distribution of wealth must remain a priority of any democratic government.

The second problem in the Middle East that has wide ramifications in society is that of education. Although Islam emphasizes knowledge and learning, the sad reality is that the standards of education are unsatisfactory. In addition, the climate for scholarship and intellectual activity is discouraging. Scholars are too often silenced, jailed, or chased out of the country by the administration. The sycophants and the intelligence services whose only aim is to tell the ruler what he would like to hear, fill the vacuum.

Education needs to be vigorously reformed. The *madrassah,* or religious school, which is the institution that provides primary education for millions of boys in the Middle East, needs to be brought into line with the more prestigious Westernized schools reserved for the elite of the land. By allowing two distinct streams of education to develop, Muslim nations are encouraging the growth of two separate societies: a largely illiterate and frustrated population that is susceptible to leaders with simple answers to the world's problems and a small, Westernized, often corrupt and usually uncaring group of elite. The third problem facing the Middle East is that of representation in the mass media. Although this point is hard to pin down, the images in the media are creating problems of understanding and communication in the communities living in the Middle East. Muslims, for example, will always complain that they are depicted in negative stereotypes in the non-Arab media. The result of the media onslaught that plagues Muslims is the sense of anger on the one hand and the feeling of loss of dignity on the other. Few Muslims will discuss the media rationally. Greater Muslim participation in the media and greater interaction will help to solve the problem. But it is not so simple. The Israelis also complain of the stereotypes in the Arab media that depict them negatively.

Muslims are aware that their religious culture represents a civilization rich in compassion and tolerance. They are aware that given a period of stability in which they can grapple with the problems of democracy, education, and self-image they can take their rightful place in the community of nations. However painful the current reality, they do carry an idea of an ideal human society with them. Whether a Turk, or an Iranian, or an Arab, every Muslim is aware of the message that the prophet of Islam brought to this region in the seventh century. This message still has resonance for these societies. Here are words from the last address of the prophet spoken to his people:

> All of you descend from Adam and Adam was made of earth. There is no superiority for an Arab over a non-Arab nor for a non-Arab over an Arab, neither for a white man over a black man nor a black man over a white man . . . the noblest among you is the one who is most deeply conscious of God.

This is a noble and worthy message for the twenty-first century in the Middle East. Not only Muslims, but Jews, and Christians would agree with it. Perhaps its essential theme of tolerance, compassion, and equality can help to rediscover the wellsprings of tradition that can both inspire and unite.

◆   ◆   ◆

This volume on Turkey by Heather Lehr Wagner introduces us to its history and society. Ms. Wagner brings out the dilemmas of Turkey confronting its European heritage on one side and its Asian heritage on the other. To Europeans, Turkey was—and is—an Islamic country. To Asians, Turkey represents a Westernized nation. This pull between the two civilizations creates Turkey's greatest dilemma, but it also gives it a unique position between them.

Few in the West realize how integrated Turkey is into Europe. It joined NATO (North Atlantic Treaty Organization) in 1952. It would have joined the European Union a long time ago, but opponents prevented it from doing so. The desire to Westernize has its critics within Turkey. Many Turks would prefer a more Islamic identity for their nation. They wish to revive the glory of the past that is associated with the Ottoman dynasty.

The author of this volume explains the legacy of the Ottomans, the rise of Kemal Ataturk, the emergence of modern Turkey, and the current situation. She does not shy away from discussing sensitive issues, such as the treatment of the Kurds. Many of the photographs from the Royal Geographical Society are being published for the first time in this book.

It is for these reasons that I congratulate Chelsea House Publishers for taking the initiative in helping us to understand the Middle East through this series. The story of the Middle East is, in many profound ways, the story of human civilization.

– **Dr. Akbar S. Ahmed**
The Ibn Khaldun Chair of Islamic Studies and
Professor of International Relations,
School of International Service
American University

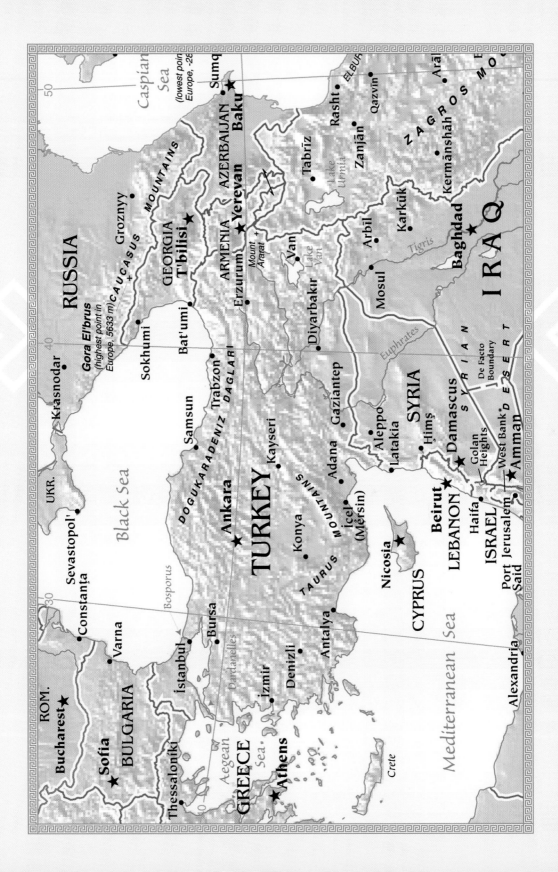

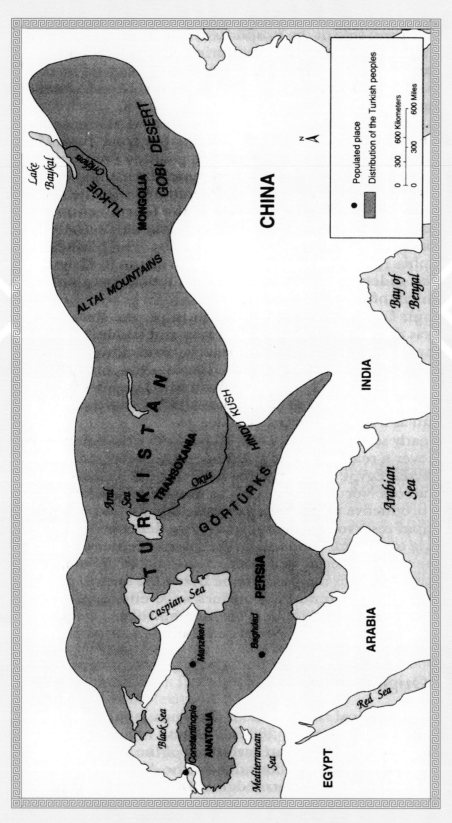

Distribution of the Turkish peoples: migrations and conquests, seventh through eleventh centuries.

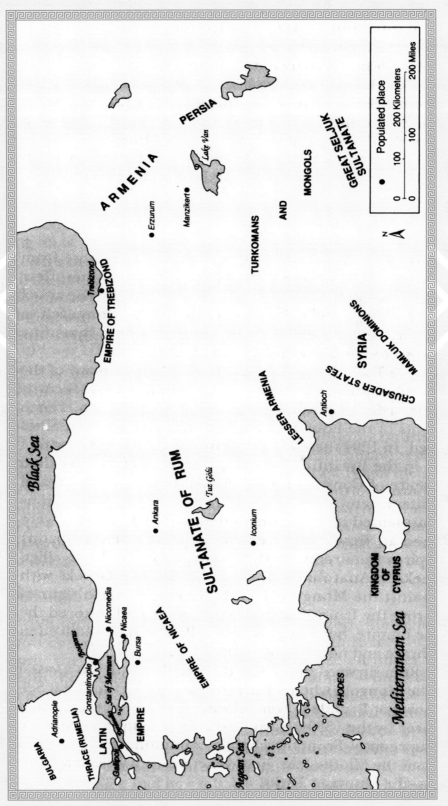

Anatolia in the thirteenth century.

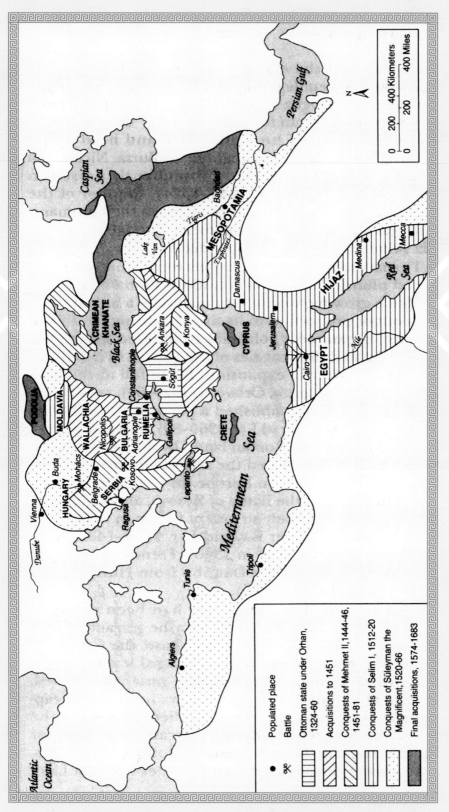

Expansion of the Ottoman Empire, 1324–1683.

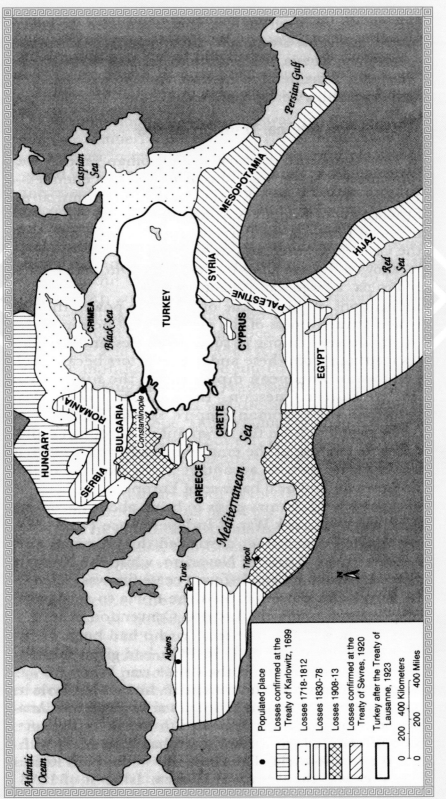

Decline of the Ottoman Empire from the Treaty of Karlowitz, 1699, to the Treaty of Lausanne, 1923.

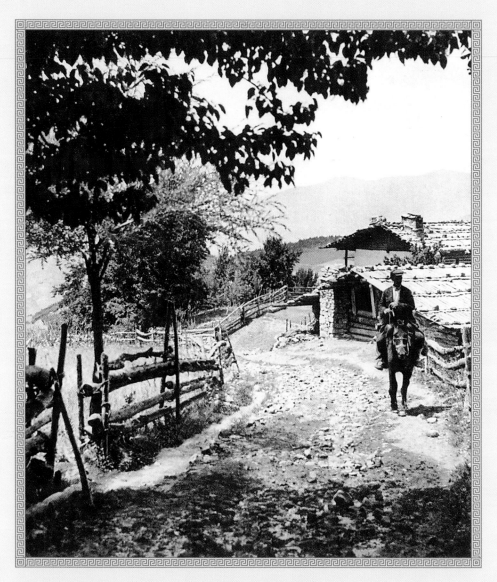

Typical Landscape and Farm, Maeander Valley, 1923

A typical village along the Maeander River in southwestern Turkey. The landscape is dotted with fig trees, olive groves, and vineyards. The river's classical name, Maeander (whence the English *meander*), is derived from its winding course.

1

The End of
the Empire

I t was very late in the evening of March 3, 1924, when frightened servants came to awaken Abdul Mejid. Mejid was the caliph, the religious leader of the new republic of Turkey, and his splendid palace reflected his position as the spiritual guide of the nation and, by tradition, of all Muslims throughout the world. The caliph, thought to be the successor to the prophet Mohammed, had served as the central link to the Muslim faith since the 11th century. Mejid enjoyed a regal lifestyle and viewed his role as caliph as a divine duty to which he was called and entitled by birth into the Ottoman royal family.

But it was a duty that had been assigned to him only two years earlier. Mejid was a quiet man who had enjoyed a fairly simple life, spending his days painting, reading books, and working in his garden, until he was named caliph. However, serving as the moral leader for 100 million Muslims was a role that required pomp and ceremony. And Mejid was happy to comply.

Each Friday—the holy day for Muslims—Mejid would race through the streets on a white horse, surrounded by guards, as the call to prayers echoed around him and the people cheered. Before praying in the mosque, Mejid was rowed across the Bosphorus Strait in an imperial barge by 14 rowers, all dressed in dazzling uniforms, while cheering crowds would line the shore awaiting his arrival.

But Mejid's choice of dazzling uniforms and showy demonstrations of faith, while entertaining to the crowds that cheered his every appearance, proved less enjoyable to the new forces governing Turkey. Mejid was a member of the Ottoman royal family, which had once ruled an empire as vast as the continental United States yet gradually seen its lands and power slip away. Mejid's cousin, the Ottoman sultan and ruler of all Turkey, had been forced out of power and out of Turkey less than two years earlier. Now, it was Mejid's turn.

On that March night, Mejid arose and discovered that Istanbul's governor and chief of police were at his palace. They informed him that the Grand National Assembly had met and, only a few hours earlier, had voted to put an end to his position as Turkey's religious leader and ordered all members of the Ottoman royal family out of the country. From now on, there would no longer be a caliph. Mejid was told to pack his things and prepare to leave the palace immediately.

A furious Mejid refused to go quietly. He ordered the governor to leave the palace at once. The police chief then informed the caliph that the palace was surrounded, the phone lines had been cut off, and the police had been given the authority to remove him by force, if necessary.

Mejid had little choice but to obey. He was told that he

and his family would be taken to the main train station in Istanbul and put on the Orient Express, a train bound for Europe. Mejid pleaded to be allowed to gather a few belongings, a request that was finally granted. Then, with two of his four wives, his son and daughter, and three staff members, he left the palace under police guard at 5 A.M. on March 4, 1924. Fearing that there might be trouble if the caliph was paraded through the streets of the densely populated city of Istanbul, the police decided to take Mejid and his family instead to Çatalca, a smaller train station outside the city. There, the heavily guarded group waited all day and into the night until at last, near midnight, the Orient Express pulled into the station. A private coach had been attached to the train. After boarding the coach, Mejid was given an envelope containing £2,000 in British currency as well as temporary papers entitling him to travel to Switzerland. In return, Mejid agreed to sign a statement indicating that he was resigning as caliph to comply with the people's wishes, and would spend his remaining years studying art.

The caliph's resignation lasted for as long as it took the train to cross over the border into Bulgaria. He then immediately issued a new statement, explaining that he had resigned only under pressure, and that he considered the Assembly's decision to be invalid. But he would learn, to his astonishment, that very few people cared. One final indignity was to be added to his hasty flight from the country his family had ruled for centuries. When the train reached the Swiss border, Mejid was held at the frontier. A Swiss law prevented immigrants with more than one wife from entering the country. It was only after a delay that he was permitted to enter his new homeland.

The remaining members of the Ottoman royal family quickly followed Mejid into exile. Only a few days later, 116 members of the dynasty were forced to leave their homes. The majority of them would never return.

THE BIRTH OF A NATION

The disappearance of the Ottoman royal family from Turkey was not a random act, a mere side effect of the shift in government from a monarchy to a republic. It was, instead, part of a careful plan to usher Turkey into the modern age, to make it a nation recognized by other world powers, and to create a new population of skilled workers, proud of their country and contributing to its wealth, not to the wealth of a royal ruler.

For the country that the caliph saw for the last time on March 4, 1924, was lying in ashes. World War I had left great devastation, the people were largely unskilled in any trade, and the collapse of the Ottoman Empire had left them vulnerable to foreign influences. Islamic religious and cultural traditions dominated the educational system and dictated much of daily life, restricting certain vital trades (shoemakers, tailors, carpenters) to non-Muslims and making the Turkish people dependent on outsiders for many basic necessities.

But the man who had assumed power in the aftermath of World War I determined to change all that. Mustafa Kemal, a respected military officer and the new president of Turkey, was a visionary who planned to shape a country that could stand as an equal with the great powers of Europe. He understood that this new republic would need an educated people, with women as well as men trained in useful skills, speaking a single language, sharing a common goal of making Turkey a strong, independent nation.

As the Orient Express carried the caliph and his family into exile, the land they left behind was changing forever. The palaces from which they fled would, for the most part, remain abandoned, their crumbling shells a haunting reminder of Turkey's past. The once-mighty Ottoman sultans would scarcely recognize the nation that would rise up from the ashes of their empire. Barely a month after the

Selling Firewood, Lake Van, c. 1894

Note the barren shores. Scarce firewood is being weighed and sold along the shoreline.

caliph's departure, the religious courts, which had used Muslim teachings to make legal decisions on matters of marriage, divorce, and inheritance, would be shut down. And more revolutionary changes would follow. Alcohol would be legalized. Women would no longer be required to wear a veil. Schools would be open to all, would be taught in Turkish rather than Arabic or Persian, and would be redesigned to educate students in Turkish history, not Islamic traditions.

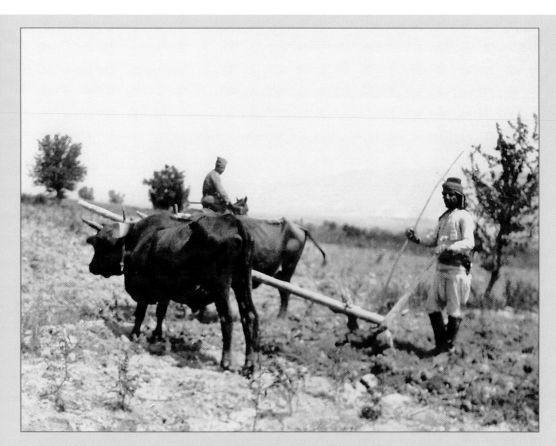

Turkish Peasant Plowing Field, Southwestern Anatolia, 1923

This armed Turkish peasant is using oxen to plow a licorice field in southwestern Anatolia. Licorice is used as an ingredient in cough lozenges and syrups, and in flavoring candies and tobacco. The herb grows about three feet tall with clusters of blue flowers. It is the root that is used commercially. A juice is made by boiling crushed licorice root. The root continues to be an export crop of southwestern Anatolia.

It would become one of the most wondrous transformations in history—one man, with a combination of extraordinary vision, exceptional instincts and great political savvy, pulling his country back from the brink of ruin and shaping it into a modern nation. At the beginning of the 20th century, Turkey was marked by loss—in war, in territory, in prestige, and in leadership. By the century's end, Turkey could be measured by its gains—membership in NATO, strategic partnerships with neighbors in Asia and the Middle East, an educated population, and women playing an active role in business and politics. The dreams Mustafa Kemal nurtured of a modern Turkey would become nearly a reality.

And yet modern Turkey still straddles two continents, sometimes drawing close to Europe, other times swinging closer to Asia. Although the caliph was forced from Turkey on that March night, the private coach did not carry away all traces of Islamic thought or heritage from the land, and its presence would be felt in the future, in revivals that threatened to sweep away Kemal's carefully structured plans and push Turkey back to an earlier age. And the fiercest battles Turkey would fight would take place within its own borders, against its own people.

For the Turkey that Kemal began to shape on that March night was his vision of a modern country—a Turkey that would turn away from its past and fix its gaze firmly to the West. His dream was for a Turkey marked by order, by Western laws and thought, by economic prosperity and a secular (rather than religious) form of government. He dreamed of a unified nation of Turkish peoples, identified simply and solely as Turks.

There was little room in this vision for the cultural identities that had shaped the Ottoman Empire for centuries. There was little room for the rich tradition and strong influence of Islam in the daily life of the people. It was, in the end, one man's vision, and when that man was gone, Turkey struggled to shape its own destiny, separate from the dreams of Mustafa Kemal.

But all of this lay far in the future on that March night that marked the beginning of a brand-new age for Turkey. The man who had engineered the caliph's hasty departure had no time for nostalgic reflection. He was hard at work, creating a new nation.

Harbor of Constantinople, 1880

Mosques, minarets, palaces, and houses line the shore of the Bosphorus Strait in this photograph of Istanbul, then called Constantinople. This view shows the European side of the Bosphorus, including the Dolmabahçe Palace (upper right), built by the Turkish sultan in 1856 with loans from foreign banks. In 1880, Constantinople was the capital of the declining Ottoman Empire.

The Revolution
Begins

 visitor to Istanbul at the beginning of the 20th century would have found a city whose days of glory seemed far behind it. The capital of the Ottoman Empire had served as a setting for many of the greatest civilizations the world had known. The Hittites had dominated the region during the Middle Bronze Age, fighting Egyptian pharaohs and battling the Greeks until losing the land to the Persians. Alexander the Great conquered the land around 300 B.C., and later came the mighty Roman Empire. The ancient city of Byzantium was rebuilt under Constantine in 300 A.D., and as the new capital city, it became known as Constantinople. An entire empire—the Byzantine Empire—spread out from this city into Asia and the Balkan Peninsula. Later, conquering Islamic dynasties moved from Mecca into the region.

By 1453, a new group had swept into Constantinople: nomadic tribesmen known as the Ottomans. Fierce warriors on horseback, they traveled across the lands, seizing territory as they headed west across Asia and on into Europe. Setting their capital in the same glittering setting that Constantine had chosen, the Ottomans created an empire that was the most powerful in the world in the 1500s and 1600s. Their territory, known as the Ottoman Empire, spread out into Asia, parts of Europe and northern Africa, and the countries known today as Iran, Saudi Arabia, Iraq, and Syria.

The Ottoman Empire had a vast international trade network, with huge shipping and extensive caravan capacity. The empire relied on slave labor, and economic growth also depended on its ability to continue to invade new lands, seize the goods, and capture new slaves. But it became increasingly difficult to govern so many different peoples, keep so many territories in line, and ensure that orders were followed while also continuing to conquer new regions.

The Ottoman Empire had known great success in medieval times, but by the 17th century, the European armies were becoming increasingly sophisticated. Developments in science and technology led to great advances in the West, advances that the Ottomans ignored or adopted too late. The Ottoman Empire had been a successful medieval power, but as the medieval age ended, the Ottomans still clung fast to the ideas and actions that had once brought them success.

Gradually, their territories slipped away. Corruption dominated the government. The sultans who ruled the empire frequently seized the throne from family members, either by murdering them or locking them away. Citizens of the empire were divided into two general classes, or groups. The upper class, which included the imperial family, wealthy landowners, and religious and

Boat with a Cargo of Juniper Wood, Lake Van, 1894

Juniper is an aromatic evergreen tree. The berry is used to flavor foods and alcoholic beverages, especially gin. The fragrant wood is used for fence posts and in making pencils.

military leaders, paid no taxes. The lower class, consisting mainly of peasants, farmers, and some craftsmen, paid taxes to support the lavish lifestyles of their rulers.

Islamic rules and religion dominated the daily life of most Ottomans. The neighborhood *mosque* (the Muslim place of worship) was the focus of daily life—boys were educated there, social activities took place there, and representatives were selected from the mosque (as well as other places of worship) to make the people's needs known to the sultan. While Islam was the chief religion, the Ottomans did allow other religious groups to flourish, and Jews and Christians lived in relative peace with their Islamic countrymen, particularly in the large city of Istanbul (also known as Constantinople).

Süleymaniye Mosque, c. 1890

Istanbul's most important mosque is both a tribute to its architect, the great Sinan (c. 1491-1588), and a fitting memorial to Süleyman I, "the Magnificent" (1520-66). It is under his rule that the Ottoman Empire reached its extent, an empire that stretched from Algiers to the Caspian Sea and from Hungary to the Persian Gulf. Süleyman's reign was a time of great artistic and architectural achievements. Sinan designed many mosques and other major buildings in Istanbul.

The Süleymaniye Mosque was not only a place of worship but also a charitable foundation. Note that the mosque is surrounded by domed buildings. Within these buildings, there was a hospital, a public food kitchen for the poor, a school, a bath-house, Islamic study halls, and a lodging space for travelers. In 1890, these buildings still functioned as intended by Süleyman. Today, though, the food kitchen has been replaced by a café—and only the Islamic study halls still operate.

Women fared less well in the strict climate of the Ottoman Empire. Men could have more than one wife, and this *harem* (the women of the household) of as many as four wives lived in a separate section of the house, emerging in public only rarely, and then always shielded from public view by a veil. The Islamic faith ruled out art that showed beings with an immortal soul, so the creative minds of the empire found artistic expression in crafts, such as the richly beautiful carpets that are, to this day, representative of the region's most impressive works of art.

But the oppressive taxes, the frequently weak sultans, the corruption and bribery that marked the military, all contributed to the loss of greatness. By the beginning of the 20th century, important territories such as Greece and Egypt had been lost. With each loss of territory, large groups of Muslim refugees would come pouring into the remains of the empire. Rumblings of independence, first having touched the people in the farthest stretches of the empire, now echoed in the streets of the capital city.

A visitor to Istanbul in those early days of the 20th century would find the seaport built on the seven hills still bustling with trade, but also with whispers of dissatisfaction. The lovely mosque *Hagia Sophia* (originally a Christian church dating back to 537 A.D.), its four minarets glistening in the bright light, would still call the faithful to prayers under its impressive dome. And the palace of the Ottoman sultans still provided an awesome symbol of the power of the once-mighty empire. But the streets of the seaport now contained rumors of revolution. The plotters were young and well connected. And the empire that had once ruled a vast stretch of the world had shrunk to a mere shadow of its former self. It was still prepared to fight threats from outside forces. But the greatest threat would soon come from within.

THE YOUNG TURKS

In the early days of the 20th century, the crumbling Ottoman Empire was ruled by the sultan Abdul Hamid. Hamid felt his power slipping away, and rather than relaxing the strength of his rule, he tightened his grip, suspending the constitution, disbanding Parliament, and using a secret police force to spy on his people and punish any who disagreed with his policies. The secret police strongly stamped out any dissidents in Istanbul, but they were less vigilant in some of the further regions of the empire.

In the port town of Salonica (now known as Thessaloniki), a region that now belongs to Greece but at the time was part of the empire and the headquarters of the Ottoman Third Army, a secret society was formed that would forever change Turkey. The Committee of Union and Progress, or C.U.P., was born in a climate of dissatisfaction and disorder in this area that made up one of the most important cities of the Ottoman Empire. The members of this new and secret party, many of whom came from the army, swore loyalty to only two things: the Koran (the holy book of the Islamic faith) and the gun. As the revolutionary fervor grew, the young soldiers who had joined the society in protest against the corruption they saw all around them were promoted to higher ranks within the army, and soon had weapons and men under their command. In addition, the conditions in Salonica were growing increasingly hazardous, as they struggled to hold the remains of the empire together with little support from the sultan. In fact, the sultan feared any possible coups from the army, and as a result kept them begging for equipment and money, as soldiers went months without pay and faced more frequent attacks with out-of-date weapons. Guerrilla groups frequently threatened the increasingly desperate troops, and these soldiers on the front lines could clearly see this portion of the empire slipping away.

And so, when the revolution came, it began not with an oppressed group of peasants, but rather from the elite itself, young captains and majors in the army who wanted not to destroy the class system but rather to be able to fulfill their leadership roles effectively, in the way they had been trained from an early age. They did not want to create a new

Raft Leaving Diarbekr, 1906

This raft-ferry crossed Lake Van from Diarbekr (Tatyan) to Van, a distance of about 40 miles. The route was used by overland travelers going from Turkey to Persia (Iran). Today, a modern ferryboat makes the same lake crossing. This photograph is of Mrs. L.E. Hopkins, who, with her husband, traveled across Asiatic Turkey and Persia in 1906.

nation—they wanted to restore their nation to its former glory, to bring back the "good old days."

By 1908, rumors of trouble had reached the Sultan's ears. At first, he dismissed them. By the time he sent out spies to assess the situation, the rebellion needed only a small spark to set the revolution in motion, and the sultan provided it. One young officer named Enver Bey was thought by the sultan's spies to be at the heart of much of the trouble. He received a suspicious note from the sultan's commissioner, asking Enver Bey to report to the capital city in order to sort out the situation and receive a promotion. Enver Bey had an idea of what the result would be of his trip to Istanbul, and instead chose to escape to the nearby hills of Resne.

Another member of the C.U.P. soon followed—Major Ahmed Niyazi. But Niyazi took with him weapons, supplies, money, and 200 men. He had no intention of surrendering quietly, as is clear in a note he wrote to his brother-in-law on the night before his escape: "I see no point in lengthy explanations. The cause is known. Rather than live basely, I have preferred to die."

But Niyazi did not die. Instead, he and his fellow revolutionaries gained in strength and numbers as news of the rebellion spread through the army. The sultan tried bribery, spying, and even harsh punishment, but it all failed. On July 21, 1908, a telegram arrived at the sultan's palace from the C.U.P. It demanded that the constitution be immediately put back into effect. If not, the message warned, the sultan's heir would be proclaimed the new sultan and an army of 100,000 men would march on Istanbul. After two days of desperate searches for a way out, the sultan realized that he had no choice. On July 24, he announced that the constitution had been restored. The Young Turks, as the revolutionaries came to be known, had won this battle. But the war was only beginning.

THE BIRTH OF A WARRIOR

Less than 30 years before the launch of the C.U.P., the town of Salonica had witnessed another birth, one that would prove equally significant in the history of the land that would become Turkey. In the winter of 1881, a young man was born to a middle-class Muslim family. In keeping with the tradition of the time of giving babies names with religious significance, he was named Mustafa, meaning "the chosen," one of the names by which the prophet Muhammad was known in the Muslim faith. The precise date of his birth

Ottoman Houses, c. 1890

The typical, fashionable townhouse of 19th-century Istanbul had a ground floor of stone above which were one or two wooden stories. Wooden lattice covers over the windows on the upper stories ensured that the women of the house were able to watch life on the street below without being seen themselves. Few wooden houses have survived. Many have been restored as hotels. Even though the law forbids their demolition, it is extremely hard to obtain insurance for them in a city that had experienced many devastating fires.

is unknown, having been recorded in a family Koran that later disappeared.

Mustafa knew tragedy early in his life. Of his six brothers and sisters, only he and a sister would survive. His father died when Mustafa was only 7 years old, and he moved with his mother and sister to his uncle's farm. But the opportunities for education were few, and Mustafa's mother decided to send him back to Salonica to live with relatives and attend school.

The city of Salonica, like much of the Ottoman Empire, was caught between two worlds as the 19th century came to a close. As European travelers and tradesmen came into the region, settling in different parts of the empire, they brought with them European ideas and progressive thoughts that frequently clashed with the traditions of Islam. In the schools of Salonica, the conflict was clear. Some parents chose to send their children to the traditional schools whose teaching was based on the Koran. But a new system of civil and military schools was operated by the state, designed to teach future government workers and military officers—these schools were considered to be more progressive and "European." In fact, before his death Mustafa's father had fought with his mother over which school their son would attend, his father preferring the more modern state school while his mother fought bitterly for the traditional neighborhood school.

In the end, Mustafa found himself in Salonica's state school, designed to prepare him for a career in government. But he was not a model student, and after being beaten by a teacher for fighting with another student, he was pulled out of the school by his grandmother. After this less-than-successful beginning, Mustafa decided that he wanted to attend the military academy, largely because he loved the stylish military uniforms the students there wore. The blonde, blue-eyed Mustafa had become vain about his appearance. The traditional Turkish costume, with baggy pants and a cummerbund that students in the civil school wore, seemed old-fashioned to him. His neighbor's son attended the military school, and Mustafa was jealous of his stylish uniform. He begged his mother to let him enroll in the military academy, but she was worried about the danger, uncertainty, and travel away from home a soldier's life would involve. She refused.

Mustafa secretly took the entrance exams and only after he was admitted did he approach his mother with his plans. She finally relented, and so her 12-year-old son began his 13 years of military education.

The military academies of the time were training an elite class, and they took the instruction seriously. Students were educated in history, economics, and philosophy, as well as military skills. The system of teaching used at the time was by rote, involving memorization. In each class, a teacher would appoint one student to serve as the "repeater," leading the class in repeating passages out loud over and over again until they had been memorized. Mustafa took on this role in the classroom, and soon became a successful student. He won sergeant stripes, became the leader of his class, and took on a second name.

He would later claim that the last name was given to him by his math teacher, impressed by his skill at solving problems. The last name *Kemal* means "perfection" in Turkish. And so, at the age of 13 or 14, the future leader of Turkey became Mustafa Kemal.

By March 13, 1899, Mustafa had completed military high school and entered the infantry class of Istanbul's War College. He was 18 years old. Despite the fact that he and his fellow students were considered an elite group of young men, preparing to defend their sultan and their empire, they suffered the kind of "boot camp" treatment common to so many new recruits. They were treated roughly by their superior officers, fed simple, basic food, expected to observe traditional Islamic rules for prayer five times a day, and allowed to read only textbooks.

After struggling to find his place at the college, Mustafa settled in and became a hardworking student, earning the post of junior sergeant in charge of his class and winning special recognition for his skill in French. The hard training would benefit Mustafa throughout his life, but more important were the contacts he formed there. For amongst the friends he made would become a core group that would fight together in the First World War and then go on to form the resistance movement that would lead Turkey into a brand new age.

THE SEEDS OF REVOLUTION

For the young cadets, the promise of great success that had once been guaranteed for those seeking a career in the military seemed less certain at the beginning of the 20th century. Rumors soon reached the ears of the students that military officers were not receiving their pay on time or at all. The signs of corruption were growing clear, as spies for the sultan were richly rewarded while those fighting to protect the empire were cheated out of their salaries. The forced exercise of calling out "Long live the Sultan" throughout the day annoyed these officers-in-training as they wondered whether their ruler would provide for them when their schooling had ended. Mustafa's expertise in French class provided him with a firm knowledge of the facts of the French Revolution, and the experience of the brave French revolutionaries he studied as they overthrew a tyrannical ruler could not help but color his perception of the world around him.

The city in which they studied, the capital city of Istanbul, was really two separate communities: the neighborhood known as *Pera*, where the Christians lived and worked, and *Stambul*, the neighborhood of the Muslims. The two communities were marked not only by their faith, but also by the history they seemed to represent. Stambul looked like a medieval city, with its palaces, its domes and minarets, a community of buildings erected in the 16th century that were slowly crumbling into decay. Women were seldom seen in the streets, and when they were, they

Street Scene, Üsküdar, 1914

Üsküdar is on the Asiatic side of the Bosphorus Strait opposite Istanbul. In 1914, the city was primarily residential. The wooden houses in this photograph were painted a variety of colors. A military hospital in the city was made famous during the Crimean War (1853-56) by the pioneering work of Florence Nightingale.

were always covered in black veils. The streets only seemed to come fully to life during the five times a day that the sound of the *muezzin* (a Muslim crier) rang out from the minarets, calling the faithful to prayer.

If Stambul seemed to represent the past, the community known as Pera was marked by its modernity. Wealthy merchants built palaces here in the Western style, and the

Interior of Hagia Sophia (Aya Sofya), Istanbul

Known as the "Church of Holy Wisdom," the Hagia Sophia is among the world's greatest architectural achievements.

In 532 A.D., the Emperor Justinian decided to build a church that would surpass the ancient Temple of Solomon. Construction took less than six years and involved more than 10,000 workers and the Eastern Roman Empire's most eminent architects. Justinian ordered that the most precious materials be used, which resulted in the further pillaging of Delphi, Athens, and Ephesus. The inauguration, held with great pomp, took place on 26 December 537 A.D.

After the Ottoman conquest of the city in 1453, the church was converted into a mosque. The Byzantine mosaics disappeared under layers of plaster. In 1935, Atatürk made the site into a museum. Not all of the plaster has been cleared, but the beauty of the space and the visible mosaics leave onlookers astonished.

Justinian's church was the first to combine the basilica layout and the dome, symbol of the celestial sphere and the Kingdom of God. The idea was such a success that all Islamic architecture is derived from it.

stores were full of the latest goods from Europe. The streets were full of foreign tourists, and the hotels, cafes, and shops were generally run by foreigners as well, who benefited from the laws that excluded them from paying any taxes.

To Mustafa and his friends, the city in which they lived

seemed to symbolize the decay of the Ottoman Empire. They, as future soldiers, would soon be asked to defend the borders from foreign invaders. But the battle seemed to have already been lost in Istanbul, where foreigners lived in wealth and comfort while the sultan's people supported the royal family with crippling taxes.

The young cadets soon decided to produce a newspaper as a way to circulate their thoughts to like-minded students. Newspapers were forbidden at the school, and it was illegal to publish anything critical of the sultan, but the group met in secret and continued to meet and publish their revolutionary writings after they finished schooling. They were eventually betrayed by a friend and briefly imprisoned. The timing was terrible, as the newly graduated officers were awaiting decisions about where they were to be posted when they were arrested. Mustafa had been hoping for a top position with one of the Ottoman armies posted in the Balkans—he would have been closer to home and in a spot where a lot of political action was taking place. But the month-long arrest meant a shift in his status; Mustafa was sent to the 5th Army, in the less desirable outpost of the empire, the city of Damascus in Syria.

Forming part of the cavalry regiment whose assignment was to police Druse tribesmen, Mustafa witnessed first-hand the poor conditions and corruption that marked the Ottoman army operating in that remote region. The army was poorly supplied, with some officers lacking boots or proper gear while operating on horseback, and there was great temptation for soldiers who were owed several months' wages to steal from the marauding tribesmen. Mustafa apparently refused to participate. He did not want money. He wanted the opportunity to do the job for which he had trained—to uphold the glory of the empire, not engage in petty stealing. He wanted to try negotiation, diplomacy, and skill to deal with the tribesmen; his superior officers viewed him as interfering, and treated him suspiciously if at all.

The city of Damascus was a grim place for the young officer. Far from the excitement of Istanbul, or the busy prosperity of his hometown, Damascus was largely untouched by modern life. Mustafa began to realize that the Ottoman Empire was its own worst enemy, its soldiers corrupt and unwilling to try anything new, its lands crippled by old-fashioned Muslim ways.

Mustafa managed to find a few friends who shared his views, and they formed a secret society—the Fatherland Society. As military assignments sent him to other parts of the region, he formed new groups in Jaffa, Jerusalem, and Beirut. The goal these officers shared was to bring about a revolution, using force if necessary. But Mustafa knew that, for the revolution to truly succeed, it had to begin not in a remote outpost of the empire but closer to its heart. He left his regiment without permission, and with the help of friends was smuggled back into his hometown of Salonica. There, other friends arranged papers that granted him a medical absence, and he was able to move about the streets of his hometown, organizing a new branch of the secret society and renaming it the Fatherland and Freedom Society, with many of his old friends from military school joining him. But his unauthorized leave soon came to the attention of the authorities, and Mustafa hurried back to Damascus, completing his posting there in 1907. The society he had founded in Salonica suffered in his absence, but its members soon found another outlet for their revolutionary ideals. A new group was being formed in the city, with goals and ideas quite similar to those of Mustafa. Its name: the C.U.P.

AN END AND A BEGINNING

By 1907, Mustafa had completed his service in Syria and, using many of his contacts, was able to arrange a posting

Fishing Weirs, Lake Van, c. 1894

Lake Van, in eastern Anatolia, is unusable either for drinking or irrigation because of its high saline content. The salt water allows for no animal or fish life except for a small highly prized carp that lives on the weedy mud bottom of the lake. The fish was caught by using a series of reed weirs that made an enclosure or trap.

back in Salonica. When he returned in the fall of that year, the whispers of revolution were growing louder in the streets of his hometown. But Mustafa found himself very much an outsider. His posting in Damascus, away from the action, meant that the revolution had, in a way, begun without him. His Fatherland society had disappeared, and although he joined the C.U.P., he found that the leaders either argued with his ideas or, worse, ignored them. So it was that when the revolution finally came, Mustafa's name is not amongst its leaders.

In fact, when the Young Turks' triumph finally came, it was to be short-lived. For a brief time the constitution was restored, people danced in the streets, and the young officers were cheered by enthusiastic crowds. But their plans for a return to the "good old days" contained little detail, beyond the restoration of the constitution. The Young Turks' patriotism could not make up for a lack of political experience. As they marched under banners proclaiming phrases like "Liberty, Equality, Fraternity, Justice," they little understood the consequences these revolutionary words would have for their beloved homeland. The justice and equality they offered were for Ottomans. The Christians, the Jews, and the ethnic minorities in various parts of the empire were offered little. It is not surprising, then, that this revolution, rather than holding the remains of the empire together, instead caused more pieces to split away, as other groups sought their dream of "liberty, equality, fraternity, and justice."

Within three months, the Ottoman region of Bulgaria declared its independence. Days later, Austria seized the Ottoman provinces of Bosnia and Herzegovina, and Crete voted to unite with Greece. The authority of older officers in the farther regions of the empire had been challenged by the Young Turks; now they found it increasingly difficult to maintain order in their outposts. The newspapers, freed from censorship by the revolution, now published complaints against the new government, criticism of the leaders and updates on the disastrous internal policies.

Mustafa, sensing the unfortunate turn of events, became a vocal critic of the Young Turks, and as a result, was sent to North Africa on a mission, largely to get him out of the way. But while he was away, the revolution was crumbling, and he returned to find the C.U.P. on the brink of disaster. The revolution had begun in Salonica, but Salonica was not the capital, and in Istanbul, public—and military—discontent with the new government grew out of control. On the night of April 12, 1909, troops that had been sent to ensure that the constitution was carried out instead launched a mutiny, joined quickly by teachers and students at various religious schools in the city. They marched into the Parliament building, forcing the officials there to flee. Within 24 hours, the sultan had agreed to their demand to appoint a new, more conservative head of government who would follow the rules of Muslim law. Members of the C.U.P. that were found were executed; the others fled the city or went into hiding.

A FORCE FROM SALONICA

The C.U.P. members in Salonica quickly gathered together an armed force to retake Istanbul. Mustafa was appointed chief of staff of one of the divisions appointed to march on Istanbul, and he feverishly set to work planning the attack. Within a week the army had established a base just outside the city, encircling the port by land while a fleet of ships surrounded Istanbul in the water. The forces quickly re-took the city, seized the leaders of the rebellion, and hanged several of them on Galata Bridge.

Because the rebellion had been supported, at least in part, by the sultan, the C.U.P. decided that the sultan must be replaced. Parliament was reconvened, and a vote was forced.

A small group of officials was sent to the sultan's palace to deliver the bad news. Recognizing it as his *kismet* (the Muslim word for fate or destiny), the sultan asked whether his life would be spared. None of the officials who had been sent knew the answer. This was too much for the sultan, who called out, "May the curse of God rest on those who have caused this calamity!" He was allowed to gather a few belongings, and then was escorted to the railway station, where a special train had been prepared. The news of his destination could not have been a comfort to the sultan. He was to be exiled to Salonica, the very place where all of his troubles had first begun.

Antalya, c. 1910

Antalya is a Mediterranean port in southwest Turkey. It was founded in the
2nd century B.C.

   At the end of World War I (1918), Italy claimed Antalya and the surrounding area
as part of the postwar division of the Ottoman Empire. Turkish nationalists drove out
the Italians in 1921. Today, the city is a highly esteemed Turkish beach resort with
broad avenues and modern buildings. Antalya, as pictured above, exists no more,
although there have been attempts to preserve what remains of the wooden houses
as an example of what an Ottoman Mediterranean village looked like.

3

An Empire
at War

While the C.U.P. had restored its power in Istanbul, it was clear that something had gone terribly wrong with its policies to allow a rebellion to flare up so quickly. Mustafa thought he knew the reason. Mixing political power and military power can be a difficult task, and in Istanbul the C.U.P. had relied too heavily on enforcing its policies through military might, rather than making sure that it had the support of the Parliament. For a party that claimed its main goal was to ensure that the constitution was followed line by line, they could not ignore the Parliament or its importance in creating a stronger empire. Similarly, it was important to make sure that military officers had a clear sense of their role, rather than forcing them to try to balance their military duties with political jobs.

Three months after the successful retaking of Istanbul, the C.U.P. held its annual meeting in Salonica. Mustafa made his first political speech there, arguing that expecting military officers to be both soldiers and politicians meant that they would fail at both jobs. A strong government would require both a strong military and a strong political party, he stated. His solution: officers would need to choose—either they would be politicians or military men, but not both.

The sensible argument impressed a few in the party, but more members saw him as a threat, rather than a spokesman. Mustafa received a request from a young party member to discuss the ideas he had expressed at the meeting. Sensing trouble, Mustafa agreed to the meeting but, when the young man arrived at his office, Mustafa casually pulled a gun from a drawer and placed it on the desk. The young officer made some feeble attempts at conversation before finally admitting that he had been sent to kill him. A second attempt occurred when Mustafa was walking in the streets of Salonica late one night. Sensing that he was being followed, he slipped into a doorway, pulled out his gun and waited. The hired killer slowed down, but then walked past.

Mustafa sensibly decided to withdraw from politics and focus on his military career. He made it clear to friends and fellow officers that the C.U.P. had slipped into the kind of party he felt was doomed to failure—one relying on secret meetings, plots and counterplots, and violent means to get rid of anyone who disagreed with their policies. But by 1911, the focus of the Ottoman Empire had slowly turned from internal political quarrels to external threats, as Germany began to flex its muscles and the threat of war loomed on the horizon. It was Italy who moved first against the Ottomans, announcing its decision to seize the Turkish provinces of Tripoli and Cyrenaica in North Africa.

Mustafa knew that an even greater threat was still to come. Austria and Russia were threatening Ottoman provinces in the Balkans. The empire could easily begin to splinter into chaos if threats surfaced on more than one border. But Mustafa was, first and foremost, a soldier. He set sail for Libya on October 15, 1911, determined to assist in the effort to defend the North African frontier from Italian forces.

He would never see Salonica again. Within a year, Greek armies had invaded the city where Mustafa had grown up. The minarets and other traces of Turkish life were pulled down. In 1917, a disastrous fire wiped out more of the buildings, and by 1923, any Muslims who remained were forced out by the Greeks. The Jewish community, which had contributed much to the wealth and success of the city, survived in much smaller numbers until World War II, when Nazis exterminated any remaining Jewish residents.

In the Salonica of today, few traces remain of the Ottoman community that had lived there for 500 years. But there is one remaining clue to the city's important role in establishing modern Turkey. Amidst the concrete apartments that line the streets, you can find a heavily guarded pink wooden house. It is the home where Mustafa lived with his mother. A plaque in front explains that this is the former home of the founder of the Turkish republic.

AN EMPIRE TORN APART

The war that began on September 29, 1911, when Italian troops marched into Tripoli, would involve the region in violent bloodshed for nearly 12 years. For one year, Mustafa fought bravely in Cyraenica against the Italian forces. By the time he returned to Istanbul in November 1912, the capital was in chaos. The region of Macedonia had been lost. Bulgaria and Serbia had fought for—and won—their autonomy. Greek forces were massing on the border. Students demonstrated in the streets outside the palace. As the Balkan forces marched into parts of European Turkey, Muslim communities fled in terror, joining the retreating Ottoman armies, rather than facing the massacres that had already been inflicted on 12,000 Muslims in Kosovo and other regions by victorious Serbian forces.

Mustafa was 32 years old, confronted with the evidence that his dreams of glory had amounted to little. He had enjoyed only small success in his military career and none at all in his political efforts. His hometown was lost to Greece, his mother and sister were refugees forced to flee their house. His country was dissolving. And his enemies were still active.

Mustafa was given the post of military attaché for the newly formed Balkan countries. While the C.U.P. struggled to keep its capital in check by installing a military dictatorship, which would prove even more oppressive and corrupt than the government it had been formed to overthrow, Mustafa was sent into exile in Sofia.

The posting provided Mustafa with his first lengthy exposure to Western life. The newly independent region was reveling in the outcome of the Balkan Wars. Parties and balls were everywhere, the Opera had frequent, glittering performances, and the people wore fashionable clothing purchased in Vienna. The Bulgarians were gracious and hospitable to the Turks they had fought only a short time ago, and Mustafa was a frequent guest at the wealthy homes in the city.

He toured the Turkish communities in Sofia, and was amazed at how superior life was there to that back in Istanbul. The Turks operated successful businesses—something that only foreigners were allowed to do in the Ottoman Empire. They were wealthy. Their women did not need to be veiled. Modern schools educated the children of these Turks, his former countrymen.

The freedom and prosperity he saw in Sofia greatly impressed Mustafa. It soon became clear that the Turkish

Byzantine Cistern, Istanbul, c. 1935

This vast underground water cistern, which has 336 columns and is more than 25-feet tall, is an excellent example of Byzantine engineering. This enormous vault was laid out during the reign of Justinian in 532 A.D., as it was essential for the Byzantines to have a huge water reserve in order to survive long sieges of the city. The Ottomans did not know of the cistern's existence for a century after their conquest in 1453. It was rediscovered after people were found to be collecting water, and even fish, by lowering buckets through holes in their basements.

community was enjoying a superior life here, in the territory that no longer formed part of the Ottoman Empire, to that which they would have enjoyed in Turkey itself. In those days and nights, moving among the glittering diplomats in the newly independent region, Mustafa began to form the plans for a modern Turkey, modeled on the Western style he saw in the streets of Sofia.

Meanwhile, back in Istanbul, the C.U.P. leadership had undertaken a series of reforms, designed to shake up the army in the wake of the defeat in the Balkan Wars. To that end, a team of experts from Germany was invited in to assist in the army reforms. Ottoman military academies soon had

German instructors training the future elite of the Empire. German officers were added to the various army units. Turkish troops were overseen by a German military mission.

It is always dangerous to give that much authority and control over armed forces to a foreign country. In this case, the timing spelled disaster for the Ottoman Empire. For the year was 1914, and on June 28 of that year, the Archduke Ferdinand of Austria-Hungary was assassinated in Sarajevo. Within a month, World War I had begun. Mustafa, from his post in Sofia, argued strongly about the dangers of siding with Germany in the war. If Germany won, Turkey would become essentially a province of Germany, and if it lost, the Ottoman Empire would disappear. But his superiors disagreed, and by the end of October a Turkish vessel, with German officers and crew on board, sailed into the Black Sea and, without warning, attacked three Russian port cities. War had been declared.

THE BATTLE AT GALLIPOLI

Although opposed to the alliance with Germany, Mustafa was eager to play a more important military role once war had been declared. After repeatedly requesting a posting on the front lines, he was ordered to return to Istanbul to assume the command of the Ottoman Empire's 19th Division. He packed quickly, and left on January 20, 1915.

By the time Mustafa returned to the capital, the Ottoman army had suffered two disastrous defeats, in Russia and Egypt. The army command seemed to be dazed and confused, and Mustafa's experience upon arriving in Istanbul certainly gave him cause for concern. He met with several officers about his new posting, but no one was able to tell him where the 19th Division he was to command was currently located, or whether it even existed. It was finally suggested that he might try the Third Army Corps, stationed at Gallipoli, where there might be plans to form such a division.

The battle for the Gallipoli peninsula would prove to be one of the most critical of World War I. The region was strategically significant, serving as an important buffer between the Aegean Sea and Istanbul. If an invading force was able to sweep across Gallipoli and into Istanbul, the Ottoman Empire would be cut off from its German allies.

Information came to the Ottomans and Germans that the British were massing troops in Egypt in preparation for an attack at Gallipoli. The English forces numbered 80,000 men. The Germans and Ottomans had only 20,000 men to defend the mountainous, 52-mile-long coastline. The German command decided to break its forces into three groups, guarding the northern, southern and central portions of the peninsula. The plan was for the smaller forces to do their best to hold off the invasion for the two or three days it would take until reinforcements could arrive. Mustafa and his troops (a strong Turkish regiment and two weaker Arab regiments) were dispatched to Maidos, toward the central section of Gallipoli, and ordered to perform drills until they received word of where the British attack would occur.

On the morning of April 25, 1915, Mustafa sent his strongest regiment out at 5:30 A.M. to practice maneuvers up one slope of the hillside at Chunuk Bair. The terrain was quite rough and Mustafa, moving ahead of his troops, was forced to get off his horse and make the trek up the hill on foot. As he and a few officers moved up the steep hill, they saw a company of soldiers racing back down towards them. When Mustafa shouted at them, asking why they were running, they screamed, "They come, they come."

Mustafa moved to the top of the hill and saw below him a line of Australian solders, moving up the hill. They were closer to him than his own troops. He ordered the retreating lookouts to turn, fix their bayonets, and prepare to fight.

The Germans had believed that the strongest British

attack would come at the northern part of Gallipoli. They were wrong. Mustafa, with his small regiment, was facing the bulk of the invading force. Finally, his soldiers, panting from the steep climb up the hill and believing that they were at the end of their drill, joined him.

Fortunately, the regiment had prepared for the training exercise with real, rather than fake, firepower. There was no time to wait for orders from the German high command. Mustafa ordered his troops to prepare to fight.

The battle raged all day and into the night. The Australians were unable to advance, but neither did they retreat back down the hill. Each side dug in, and the fighting continued for weeks, with heavy losses on both sides. Reinforcements arrived on both sides, but the Germans remained cautious, unwilling to send a significant portion of troops anywhere for fear that the British would attack the peninsula at another point and move on to Istanbul.

On three separate occasions over the next several long, hot months, English forces attempted to take the peninsula. In three fierce battles and many bloody skirmishes, Mustafa and his troops held them off. Finally, in December 1915, the English gave up and left the peninsula. Mustafa and his troops had held the peninsula and saved Istanbul.

A FORGOTTEN HERO

Mustafa returned to Istanbul, having played a critical role in saving the Gallipoli peninsula and Istanbul itself. There were victory parades to salute the victorious Ottoman forces, but it was the sultan who was cheered as the *Ghazi* (victorious warrior) and the C.U.P. leaders and senior generals who stood high on the royal platform overlooking the parade. Mustafa's achievements were overlooked, his name was omitted from official decrees honoring the victorious soldiers, and he was largely ignored upon his return to the capital.

It must have been a bitter moment for the ambitious commander whose troops had held off the invading force for so many months. He lingered in the capital only for a few weeks for a much-needed sick leave before being dispatched to lead a corps in eastern Turkey defending the empire against an advancing Russian army. The region Mustafa had been sent to was in Eastern Anatolia, where the C.U.P. government had forced all the Armenian citizens out of their homeland based on a suspicion that they were secretly helping Russian forces.

This action remains one of the sorriest chapters in Turkey's history. The Armenians had occupied the eastern region of Anatolia for many centuries before the Turks arrived as conquerors. At the time that World War I began, approximately two million Armenians were living in the Ottoman Empire.

The Armenians were proud of their culture and heritage. The Armenian nation was the first to make Christianity its state religion, and throughout their history as a conquered people they were viewed as ideal citizens— loyal and hard-working.

But with the rise of the Young Turks to power, the Armenians were subjected to intense discrimination. The Armenians managed much of the trade and were often better educated than their Turkish neighbors. This difference in religious beliefs (Armenians were Christian), class and status sparked resentment and anti-Armenian violence soon followed.

With no support coming from the government, the Armenians took their cause to London, Paris, Geneva, and even to the hated enemies of the Turkish people—the Russians. They began promoting their own demands for independence, as well as publicizing the violent discrimination they had experienced.

Armenian Peasants, Van, 1894

It is estimated that about 2 million Christian Armenians lived within the Ottoman Empire in the 1890s. About 1.5 million of these people lived in eastern Anatolia. These Armenians, mostly peasants, lived in areas dominated by Turks and Kurds. In no province did they constitute either a majority or a plurality. There were Armenian communities in most major Anatolian towns and in Istanbul itself.

The Armenians, encouraged by Russia, began promoting Armenian territorial autonomy in eastern Anatolia. The resulting persecutions led by Turkish troops and Kurdish tribesmen killed thousands of Armenians (1894-96). The lack of death records makes a final figure impossible.

Toprak Kalesi, Near Iskenderun c. 1925

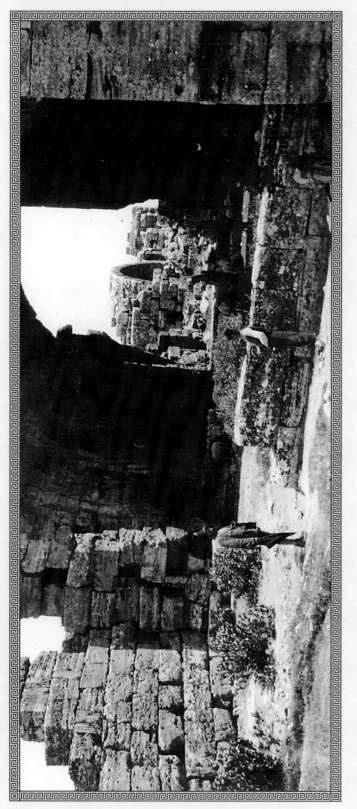

Toprak Kalesi was Cilicia's most important castle. Located in southern Anatolia, the kingdom of Cilicia, or Lesser Armenia, was established by emigrating Armenians in the 12th century. The kingdom was important for its place in the route of Venetian and Genoese trade with the East. It was conquered in 1375 by the Muslim Mamluks.

The castle was built in the 13th century. The highpoint of the ruins is the "watchpath" (pictured above), which is supposed by a series of vaulted rooms that were used as warehouses and stables. From the ramparts, there is a view of the famous Issus Plain where Alexander the Great defeated the Persian armies under Darius III in 333 BC. This is considered a decisive battle in world history as it enabled Alexander to unite Persia with the Greek world.

Armenian Eastern Orthodox Bishops and Ecclesiastics, Akhtamar, 1894

Akhtamar is an island in Lake Van, the largest inland body of water in Turkey. The lake is located in eastern Anatolia, near the border of Iran.

Akhtamar is the site of the 10th-century Armenian Eastern Orthodox Church of the Holy Cross. This church was in almost continuous use until the persecution of the Armenians in Turkey (1915-18).

The Armenian Eastern Orthodox Church is an Eastern-rite member of the Roman Catholic Church. The Armenians converted to Christianity about 300 A.D. and were the first people to do so as a nation. The liturgy continues to be celebrated in the classical Armenian language.

This photograph was taken by G.P. Devey, the British Vice-Consul in Van. His images are indispensable for understanding the peoples and places in this remote area during the 1890s.

Armenian Family, Western Anatolia, 1902

The photograph of the Armenian family was taken by Ellsworth Huntington (1876-1947), an indefatigable American traveler who wrote several dozen popular books on geography. In 1902, the Royal Geographic Society awarded him the prestigious Gill Memorial Medal "for his remarkable journeys."

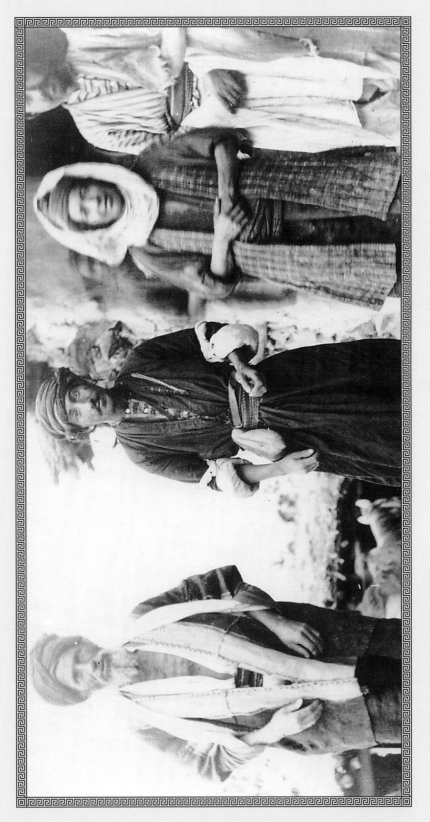

This would have disastrous consequences. As World War I broke out, the C.U.P. held a series of meetings calling for the removal of the Armenian population to a different location, under the pretense of eliminating the risk of foreign influences—particularly Russian—during a time of war. But this "evacuation" was a sham. From mid-June to late August of 1915, a horrible massacre took place. First, Armenian men were ordered to report to a central location, where they were briefly jailed and then shot. Next came the women, elderly, and children. They were ordered to march, carrying a few possessions, for hundreds of miles, heading for the desert or the mountains. Many died along the route, from thirst, hunger, exhaustion, or exposure. As the routes of these marches were followed over and over again, later victims would encounter the unburied bodies of those who had gone before.

The Turks would later claim that the Armenians were helping the Russians, serving as spies or smuggling weapons. There is little concrete evidence to support this.

But one fact is clear: in that summer of 1915, approximately one million Armenians were killed. Over half of them were women and children.

The brutal removal of this large group of citizens left the region bleak and marked by violence. To make matters worse, hundreds of thousands of Muslim refugees, many of them Kurds, soon raced into the region, fleeing the armies of invading Russians. By the time Mustafa had arrived, the streets were empty of businesses and instead filled with desperate Kurd refugees looking for food. The rough winter that followed made matters worse, as the Ottoman troops faced brutal conditions without the proper clothing or supplies. It was becoming clear that the Ottomans were fighting a losing battle.

Mustafa would go on to lead other troops in other parts of the Empire, and by the end of the war desperately attempted to hold off British forces in Palestine. But the Ottoman armies were tired, and so it was that on October 30, 1918, an armistice was signed between the Ottoman Empire and their Allied foes. Part of the empire had been lost, and many men gave their lives. The C.U.P.'s main leaders, including many of those who had engineered the disastrous entry into the war, fled for Berlin.

A new government was formed without the C.U.P., but it would merely oversee the end of the empire. Ottoman hopes that signing an armistice would mean the removal of the Allied armies were quickly shattered. British troops moved in to occupy Mosul in the portion of the empire that we now know as Iraq. Mustafa's forces in Syria were greeted with the news that British troops would soon be moving in to occupy their territory. Mustafa asked if he could form small battalions to resist the invasion. He was instead ordered back to Istanbul. He returned to the capital to the depressing sight of 55 Allied warships dropping anchor in the harbor outside the sultan's palace.

AN END AND A BEGINNING

For the next several months, Mustafa witnessed the oppressive reality of enemy troops occupying the once-glittering capital. The Ottoman Empire had been broken into pieces, and Syria, Palestine, Egypt, and Arabia had all been lost. All that was left was Turkey, and it was suffering at the hands of its invaders. The sultan dissolved the Parliament and, determining that his best chance of saving himself and Turkey lay in cooperation, immediately agreed to all of the Allied forces' demands.

For six months, Mustafa watched in despair as his country struggled under foreign control. But then, rumors of resistance in outposts in Anatolia reached English ears. The British forces suspected that Mustafa was somehow

The Theatre, Pergamum, 1923

The ancient Hellenistic city of Pergamum became the capital of the Roman province of Asia. The theatre is perhaps the best preserved of any from the ancient world. It consists of 78-stepped terraces whose incline is nearly vertical, dropping from a height of 165 feet.

This photograph was taken by Elizabeth Ness, the first woman to become a Council member of the Royal Geographical Society. Her explorations of Central Africa, and her travels from Beirut across the Syrian Desert to Persia, are described in *Ten Thousand Miles in Two Continents* (1929).

involved, and decided to arrest him. At the same time, the small rebellions could not go unchecked. The sultan proposed sending Mustafa as his representative, to deal with the situation, put a halt to any remaining gatherings of the C.U.P. and ensure that any remaining troops disbanded. For several days, the British and the sultan argued back and forth—should Mustafa be arrested for his suspected role in the rebellion in Anatolia, or instead sent to put a stop to it? Finally, the decision was made. The arrest papers were torn up and Mustafa was appointed Inspector-General of the Northern Area and Governor-General of the Eastern Provinces.

Mustafa left immediately with a few of his closest friends. As they traveled north, they learned that the Allies had agreed to allow Greece to occupy Smyrna (now Izmir) in Turkey. It was clear that, without quick action, their homeland would disappear into small provinces divided amongst the victorious Allied forces. Mustafa and his men determined that resistance, not cooperation, was the answer. Somehow, their decision reached the sultan, who quickly sent word to the British that he had made a mistake in promoting Mustafa. But he was too late. Efforts to stop Mustafa before he reached his post never made it through. He escaped only by hours.

From his new post in Anatolia, Mustafa set to work at organizing pockets of resistance. He gathered together as many of the former army corps commanders as he could. Now unemployed, these officers quickly joined Mustafa's team. He went from village to village, preaching the need for resistance to the English, explaining that they could no longer rely on the sultan to protect them, that instead they must begin to rely on themselves. He helped organize local towns and villages to enlist volunteers.

The sultan soon learned that Mustafa, rather than wiping out the resistance, was fanning its flames. He immediately ordered him back to Istanbul, but Mustafa refused to return to the capital. The sultan immediately fired him, and Mustafa in turn resigned from his army post.

Mustafa was now free to act as a civilian, and act he did. His campaign expanded from a military to a political one, as a congress of delegates was gathered together to lay out their plans for a national government, independent of Istanbul.

Door of the Monastery of Rumi, Konya, 1925

Konya is a city in central Turkey. It is considered one of the oldest urban centers in the world, dating back to the 3rd century B.C. According to legend, Konya was the first city to rise after the Great Flood that destroyed humanity.

The *tekke* ("monastery" or "lodge") consists of several buildings that included the tomb of Jalal ad-Din ar-Rumi (c. 1207-1273). He was the greatest Sufi poet and theologian who influenced Muslim mystical thought and literature. His disciples continued his work. Although Atatürk ordered this mystical Islamic sect dissolved in 1925, it still exists today.

Mustafa's opening speech before the gathered crowd made clear his plans for Turkey—there would be a revolution that would focus on the rights of the nation and the will of its people. It would create a government based on the rights of the majority, not an elite few. It was to be a government of the people and for the people, based on the principles of

Western democracy Mustafa had studied for many years.

The sultan's next move was a clever one. He dismissed the old government and called for new elections, in which the majority of the votes were won by members of the congress Mustafa had formed. As the newly elected members of Parliament, they moved to Istanbul to serve their aims within the capital—all but Mustafa, who distrusted the sultan and felt that revolution, not cooperation, was necessary. The British, tired of the resistance they were meeting throughout the Turkish countryside, gathered in the capital for a single show of force. They marched into Istanbul, occupied the city, and arrested as many of the Parliament members as they could find. The Sultan stood behind British actions, and now used his position as the head of the Muslim faith as well as the royal leader of the nation. He ordered his priests to preach messages of cooperation and support, rather than revolt. From town to town and village to village, government officials and religious leaders encouraged the local citizens to support their sultan, while Mustafa and his fellow "Nationalists," as they were now being called, spoke passionately of the need for a strong Turkey, without foreign intervention.

The result is not surprising. The country split in two, and a bitter civil war began with divisions drawn between neighbors and sometimes even between members of the same family. The sultan issued a royal decree that was sent throughout the countryside. Mustafa Kemal was an outlaw, the decree stated. He must be found and killed. Whoever did so would be performing a holy duty, and would be richly rewarded.

Turkish Peasants, Eastern Anatolia, 1935

Atatürk attempted to modernize Turkey through the clothing worn by its people. In 1925, laws were passed banning wearing the fez for men and wearing the veil for women. Nevertheless, some Turks opposed wearing Western attire for religious reasons. In the late 20th century, with the rise of Islamic fundamentalism, Western style of dress again became a subject of controversy. The government responded by imposing fines on women who wore headscarves as a Muslim gesture.

Today, many rural Turkish women still preserve traditional dress. In some areas, it is possible to identify a woman's village and her marital status from her costume. Village women have never worn a veil, but they have traditionally covered their heads and mouths with a large scarf.

4

Birth of
a Nation

For months, the fighting raged throughout the country. Quickly, foreign forces took advantage of the chaos to move in and make their own claims for territory. The Greeks moved in from their base in Smyrna. The French seized land in the south. The Kurds revolted in the east.

And then came the San Remo Conference. From April 19 to 26, 1920, representatives from the Allied forces gathered together to determine how they would divide up the Ottoman Empire. The result was the Treaty of Sèvres, a document designed to formalize the peace terms agreed upon for the region, but which really meant that the Empire would be divided amongst its conquerors into series of tiny states managed by Europeans. The lost territory would include the Arabian regions to be given to the British and French, Thrace and eight Turkish islands in the Aegean to the Greeks, and the Dodecanese Islands to Italy. Most of Anatolia would be divided into French and Italian territories. Much of Armenia would be granted its independence. The Kurds would be granted autonomy in their portion of the East. The waterways—the keys to Turkey's trade and financial survival—would be placed under Allied control. The Turkish army would be reduced to a small force overseen by the Allies, and the Turkish police would be placed under foreign control.

The response from the people was immediate—this document would mean the end of life as they had known it, and the end of their nation. The small pockets of rebels who had supported Mustafa in his calls for independence quickly swelled in numbers as more and more outraged citizens joined them. The Allies decided that the nationalist forces must be wiped out, and authorized the Greek armies to march east and north to stamp out any Ottoman troops resisting the planned partition. Of all the European forces, the Greeks were the ones most hated by the Turkish people. The Allies could not have selected a worse choice to police their new agreement, as the sight of Greek soldiers marching into their towns would virtually guarantee that the people would rise up in protest.

At first the Greeks, with the support of the Allies plus their superior numbers and weaponry, enjoyed success in their invasion. But then Mustafa turned for help to an unlikely source. The Russians and Turks had fought each other at least once a generation for centuries, most recently on opposite sides during World War I. But the Russians viewed the revolutionary movement in Turkey as an extension of their own recent revolution, and they publicly supported the efforts of Mustafa and his fellow nationalists.

Yörük Woman Spinning, Western Anatolia, 1925

The Yörük, a nomadic people from Central Asia, live in various parts of Anatolia, especially in the area called the Troad, the land around the ancient city of Troy in northwestern Asia Minor. They are known for their distinctive rugs made in many bright colors with simple patterns. A Yörük rug is hand woven using hand-spun wool and natural dyes.

Curiously, although the Yörük are Muslims, they also have animist beliefs, dominated by the idea that all nature—animal, plant, rock, or stream—is living and thinking. The Yörük consider Mount Ida a sacred place. Each year, they hold a festival on the summit, choosing a Christian date for it—August 15, the day of the Assumption.

Mustafa sent a delegation to the Russians, requesting Russian support and supplies. The request was granted.

Aided by fresh supplies, the Turk forces gained in strength, just at a point when the Greeks were weakened by leadership changes and the loss of support of a public grown weary of wars. By late 1922, the tide had turned and the Turk armies were pushing Greek forces back across the territory they had seized a short time before. As the Greeks retreated, they were joined by retreating French and Italian forces. Only the British were left and finally they, too, agreed to restore independence in Istanbul. The Treaty of Lausanne was signed on July 24, 1923. It restored all of the lands that make up modern Turkey to this day. It removed the hated peace terms that had sparked the revolution. More importantly, it officially recognized the demands Mustafa and his fellow nationalists had made, both militarily and politically. It was a victory for Mustafa, and yet there was one final matter to be settled before he could set to work rebuilding the nation. For the Allies invited two official groups from Turkey to participate in the official signing of the Treaty of Lausanne: the nationalists and the government of the sultan.

No longer could Turkey be divided. The nationalists had a clear plan for the future of their country—one that involved economic and scientific efforts to ensure Turkey's place in the community of nations as an equal. It was a time for strong leadership, under a single leader with a clear vision. Mustafa was determined to be that leader.

The solution seemed clear. The sultan had traditionally played two key roles: he had served as both the political leader of his nation and the *caliph*, the religious leader of the Muslim faith, thought to be a descendant of the prophet Mohammed himself. Mustafa wanted the position of political leader for himself. The sultan could, however, retain the role of caliph and carry on as spiritual leader for his people.

On November 1, 1922, the National Assembly passed a resolution stating that it was the position of the Turkish people that the system of government based on rule by a member of the royal family had ended on March 16, 1920 (two and a half years earlier). The resolution also stated that the role of caliph should belong to a member of the royal Ottoman family, but that the Assembly would choose which member of that sovereign family had the necessary "learning and character" to best qualify them for the position.

The sultan did not wait for the Assembly to decide whether or not his learning and character qualified him to serve as caliph. A mere 11 days after the resolution passed, the sultan fled his palace and boarded a British warship bound for Malta. His cousin, Abdul Mejid, was named as the new caliph. Never again would a member of the Ottoman royal family rule over Turkey and, as we learned at the beginning of this book, they would not perform the function of caliph for much longer, either.

A MODERN WOMAN

In the spring of 1923, Mustafa was beginning the steps that would transform Turkey into a modern nation. In the Western nations he had visited, he had been impressed by the freedom women enjoyed, and by the contributions they in turn made to their nations. He determined that, in a modern Turkey, women would enjoy many of the same freedoms as men, no longer being segregated in their homes and in the streets. One young woman named Latife, who was working as his secretary, had made a particularly strong impression on the new leader. She came from a prosperous merchant family, spoke French fluently and had studied law in Europe.

Mustafa proposed to Latife, and she quickly accepted. The wedding symbolized the kind of modern relationship Mustafa hoped for. In traditional Muslim weddings, the bride and groom do not see each other until after the wedding; the actual ceremony is performed by representatives for each side. Instead, Mustafa and Latife were married at her father's home, seated side by side at a table as they spoke their vows. In another break with tradition, Latife did not wear a veil over her face.

For their honeymoon, Mustafa took Latife on a tour of southern Anatolia. It was more of a political tour than a romantic interlude. They traveled through major cities, and Latife stayed with Mustafa (rather than in the *harem*—the part of the house set aside for women—as tradition would have dictated). She gradually began appearing without the veil, at first sparking great shock but gradually inspiring other Turkish women to shed the symbol of inferiority and lower status.

Mustafa emphasized, on this political campaign, not only his wife's equal status with him, but his equal status with his people. He mixed with the people, avoiding wherever possible any elaborate and formal ceremonies. In one instance, golden thrones were provided for Mustafa and Latife to observe a fireworks display. He sent them away, requesting ordinary chairs placed within the crowd of people who had gathered.

Mustafa's plans called for a complete break with the Ottoman Empire, with the elaborate ceremonies and strict separation of elite classes and everyday citizens. Mustafa's vision for his country was of a republic, whose government belonged to the people, and whose national assembly would serve as the people's representatives. It was a radical idea for a nation who had known centuries of royal rule. No more would their fate be left in the hands of a sultan or caliph. They would govern themselves, through that national assembly and through a president elected by that assembly.

The first step toward this new nation required a new base for governing the nation, removed geographically and symbolically from the old capital of the sultan. On October 13, 1923, the constitution was amended to indicate that the new capital of the new Turkish state would be

Turkish Villagers, 1923

The typical Turkish peasant dress before the clothing reforms imposed by Atatürk in the 1920s. Generally, most Turkish men, including peasants, have adopted European male dress. Jeans and sweatshirts are more common now than these traditional Turkish baggy trousers. Nevertheless, the traditional trousers are still worn in very rural areas. However, the cummerbund and colorful waistcoat are rare. In the 1950s, French fashion designers popularized the cummerbund style and it has now become part of men's elegant evening wear in the West.

Ankara, not Istanbul. Ankara was located in the very heart of Turkey, with none of the links to the sultans of centuries past that marked the streets of Istanbul.

But a more radical change would come only a few days later. For based in the new capital city would be a brand-new form of government. On October 29, 1923, the news was proclaimed, following approval by the assembly, that

Turkey would become a republic. Its new president, elected unanimously by 158 votes, was Mustafa Kemal.

NEW LAWS FOR A NEW REPUBLIC

Over the next few years, Mustafa would begin a series of radical reformations that would sweep away the vestiges of Ottoman thought and replace them with modern planning. The first involved removing the remaining trace of the Ottoman royal family by abolishing the need for a caliph. No more would there be confusion about whose policies would dictate life in Turkey. Next, the separate religious schools and colleges were closed, followed by the closure of the courts in which judges trained in holy laws had made judgments on legal matters based on their interpretation of the Koran.

Mustafa had become expert in the art of revolution, first carrying out a military revolution, followed by a political one. But now, as president, he began a series of symbolic revolutions, designed to transform Turkey into a contemporary society. Mustafa believed in the wisdom that you can "judge a book by its cover," and so he turned to transforming his people into a modern society not only internally, through new thoughts and beliefs, but externally, through their clothing. Specifically, their hats.

For 100 years, Muslims in Turkey were identified by the *fez*, a tall, red, cone-shaped hat adorned with a black tassel. The shape and design was important, since it allowed Muslims to touch their foreheads to the ground in prayer, as required by their faith. It also told the knowledgeable observer something about the rank and profession of the wearer.

The fez became outlawed on November 25, 1925. Men were required to wear Western-style hats; anyone wearing a fez could be arrested. Shortly thereafter, women were

Drying Tobacco, Izmir, 1930

In this photograph, tobacco is being dried. The leaves have been strung together using a needle, leaving them looped and tied to a pole. Care must be taken in this sun-dried curing process to prevent the leaf from breaking. This process is a most delicate one, especially for Turkish aromatic tobacco, as the leaf cannot be burned by the sun.

discouraged from wearing the veil. Women in cities soon stopped covering their faces, although in more remote regions they continued to wear the veil. Public employees were required to wear suits made by local merchants from local cloth, and school uniforms in Western style were also regulated.

From clothing, the reforms moved on to the way Turks measured time. In a radical step for a Muslim country, the Christian calendar was introduced, using dates based on the Christian system of measuring time before and after Christ's death, using B.C. and A.D., as well as the 24-hour measurement of daily time popular in Europe.

The speed of these transformations is truly remarkable.

The Main Street Looking East Toward the Byzantine Citadel, Ankara, 1925

Ankara lies at the bottom of a secluded valley in the center of the high and arid plateau of central Anatolia. It is difficult to imagine that this large bustling city was home to only about 30,000 people at the beginning of the 20th century. The change took place in 1923 when Atatürk decided to transform it into the capital of the young Turkish nation. The choice symbolized Atatürk's determination to tap into the most ancient origins of the new nation. The new Ankara was born: a modern dynamic city with all of the facilities and problems of a major metropolis.

Ankara, whose ancient name is Angora, gave the famous wool its name. The long-haired wool, which the city continues to produce, is renowned for its silky feel. Angora goats still roam the neighboring hills.

The modern society that Mustafa envisioned rapidly became a reality, and it is difficult to imagine how quickly life changed for his people. Pulling a nation back from the threat of political destruction is a brilliant feat; changing the way its people think about themselves and their culture is almost impossible. And yet Mustafa was able to achieve both.

Next, Mustafa began his transformation of the role of women in Turkish society. For centuries, women had enjoyed little freedom in the Ottoman world. In Istanbul, women were not allowed to walk in the street or drive in a carriage with a man, even if he was their husband. If husband and wife went outside together, the husband had

Birth of a Nation

---

to walk several steps ahead of his wife, ignoring her. Men and women did not go out together socially. On boats and trains there were separate sections for men and women, divided by a curtain. In the theater, Muslim women were not allowed to act in plays—the female parts were played by men. Women could only attend the theater on certain, special "ladies days" where the audience was reserved solely for women. Women occupied a separate, inferior world in Ottoman society, where they lived apart, in separate quarters, and rarely left the confines of their homes.

By early 1926, Mustafa had overseen a further step in his platform of increased rights for women. Divorces would no longer be granted simply because the husband wished to end the marriage. Polygamy (marriage to more than one woman) was outlawed. New inheritance laws ensured that women would receive as much as men, changing the old Muslim law that dictated that female heirs could only receive half as much as their brothers did. In the past, women could only teach in all-girls schools; now they were allowed to teach in all elementary and middle schools. Women could now pursue careers in medicine and law. And, in a controversial challenge to the religious establishment, Muslim women were now legally allowed to marry non-Muslim men, and all adults were legally granted the right to change their religion if they wished to do so.

These laws represented a significant break with the past. They were an amazing set of changes, and these swift ends to long-established customs were not always popular. But as Mustafa himself said, "The civilized world is far ahead of us. We have no choice but to catch up."

It is ironic that Mustafa, recognized as a champion of rights for women in Turkey, was less successful at his own efforts to maintain the modern marriage that had been an early symbol of the new society he planned. His marriage with Latife did not last long. Although both Mustafa and

Latife seemed to be models of the new roles for men and women in a modern Turkey, they were caught in the same struggles that would grip Turkey as it adapted to a changed society. Latife viewed herself as a partner, an equal, yet was unhappy and jealous when Mustafa's social and political gatherings expanded to include women as well as men. Mustafa, in turn, as leader of the new republic also wanted to be leader in his own home. The clash was inevitable. Mustafa ended the marriage before the new laws benefiting women went into effect. Their marriage had been a symbol of Western ceremony, but their divorce followed the Muslim tradition. Mustafa simply said, "Leave the house. I do not wish to see you any more," and the marriage was legally ended.

REELECTION AND REFORM

By 1927, Turkey's transformation was firmly underway, and a new round of elections in August and September of that year brought victory for Mustafa's Republican People's Party. He was reelected president, and shortly after the election delivered a momentous speech that has become an important part of modern Turkish history. Known simply as the *Nutuk* (speech in Turkish), it is a history—Mustafa's history—of the birth of modern Turkey. Step-by-step, it is a retelling of Mustafa's story from the moment when he landed at Samsun on May 19, 1919. The speech took 36 hours to deliver, stretched over six separate gatherings from October 15 to 20. It ended with a stirring call to the young people of Turkey, urging them to defend the republic and its independence, no matter what. This portion of the speech is, to this day, memorized as a requirement in Turkish schools.

The role of religion was further diminished in Turkey with an amendment to the constitution. Since the first Ottoman constitution of 1876, the words "The religion of the Turkish state is Islam" had clearly defined the critical importance Muslim thought and laws played. But on April 10, 1928, a law was passed which removed that phrase from the constitution. The act did not guarantee freedom of religion, but rather defined Turkey's laws and government as secular, rather than religious.

There was one additional reform Mustafa needed to make to ensure that Turkey would be more closely connected to its neighbors to the West, rather than to the East. Turkey's alphabet was Arabic with 28 letters, quite different from the Latin alphabet with 26 letters that is used in Western languages. By August, a new alphabet had been created, based on Latin rather than Arabic letters. Mustafa then set out on a tour of the country, meeting his people in schoolrooms, town halls and cafes to stress the importance of learning to read and write using this new alphabet. On November 3, a law was passed making it illegal to use the Arabic alphabet after the end of the year.

This is another remarkable example of the changes Turkey experienced under the leadership of Mustafa Kemal. Imagine what it would have been like to live during that time, when so much of what was familiar was disappearing. The way you dressed, the alphabet you used to read and write, even the clocks and calendars used to measure time, all changed. Mustafa had used his vision, his political power and his will to shape a brand-new world from the ashes of the Ottoman Empire.

A NEW ECONOMIC POLICY

In October 1929, the Great Depression struck, setting off an international set of economic crises. Turkey suffered, as the prices for Turkish agricultural exports fell in response to the monetary crises. While the economies of the West— based on capitalist principles—struggled, the state-supported

Temple of Artemis, Sardis, c. 1930

Sardis, near present-day Izmir, was the capital of the ancient kingdom of Lydia (7-6th century B.C.). Sardis was the first city to mint gold and silver coins. Croesus, the last Lydian king, was renowned for his great wealth. He surrendered to the Persians in c. 546 B.C.

Sardis became a rich city, drawing wealth from the gold, which ran through the Pactolus, a small river flowing down the slopes of the Tmolos (Boz Dagi). Croesus (561-c. 546 B.C.) had a foundry built at the foot of the mountain on a spot just before the Pactolus joins the Hermos River. Nearby, he had constructed the Temple of Cybele (later Artemis), the goddesses who were held accountable for the purification of the metal. Coins, jewelry, statuary for temples, and priceless treasures from Lydian workshops were exported throughout the ancient world.

This photograph is of the ruins of the great Temple of Artemis, considered one of the Seven Wonders of the Ancient World. Note the Ionic capitals. This structure was built in the 300s B.C. on the foundations of Croesus' temple. The Temple of Artemis was destroyed by the invading Goths (c. 260 B.C.) and was never rebuilt. Recent excavations have revealed traces of both Croesus' and three earlier temples.

industries of Russia churned briskly along. It is not surprising that Turkey decided to experiment with an economy based less on capitalist principles and more on government-sponsored industries and businesses. While the government would not interfere in agriculture, Mustafa decided to test out a five-year plan in which the state would develop certain industries, such as textiles, paper, glass, iron, steel and chemicals. While this much-needed funding (from the Turkish and foreign governments) guaranteed the development of certain important businesses, the experiment was largely unsuccessful, in part because Turkey's greatest resource—its agriculture community—was not part of the experiment, and in fact suffered as more workers were directed to the cities for industrial jobs.

The year 1933 marked a 10-year anniversary for the Turkish republic. Mustafa had been re-elected for a third term as president. But as Turkey pressed ahead on the path carved out by its leader, the world was changing. Hitler had risen to power in Germany. As the global community sought to maintain peace through the efforts of the League of Nations, Mustafa pushed ahead with more reforms.

A new legal, weekly holiday was introduced in 1935, which was to occur from 1 P.M. on Saturday to Monday morning. The concept of a holy day of rest was not a Muslim custom, as it is in the Christian and Jewish faiths. And the traditional Muslim day of worship is Friday, not Sunday—a day not for rest but rather for bustling trade, particularly in the markets located around the mosque, and public prayer. But a new law changed the day of rest to Sunday, bringing Turkey into line with other Western countries.

That same year brought an even greater change for the people. By January 1, 1935, all Turkish citizens were legally required to take a last name. Prior to this point, the Turks, like many Muslims, did not use last names. A child would be given a first name, and then known by that plus his father's first name to show the family to which they belonged. Military cadets were generally identified by their first name and their place of birth. People of status often had honorary titles added to their names. But the new law

Harvesting at the Foot of Mount Ararat, 1935

These Turkish peasants are harvesting grain on the Dogubayazit Plains in eastern Anatolia. Mount Ararat is in the background. This volcano, dormant since 1840, is the highest peak in Turkey. Ararat is traditionally associated with the mountain on which Noah's Ark came to rest at the end of the Flood.

changed all that. While military titles were kept, all other honorary or royal titles were eliminated; only the words *Bay* (Mr.) and *Bayan* (Miss or Mrs.) were to be used.

This decision resulted in some short-term chaos, as each citizen chose a last name, some reflecting a special place or name that had significance for them. Soldiers frequently chose as their last name a place where an important battle had been fought. Others chose names that reflected their trade or business. Some chose adjectives that appealed to them, and names like Rock, Steel, and Iron were particularly popular. Members of the same family frequently chose different last names.

Mustafa himself thought long and hard about the name he should choose, a name befitting the leader of the republic. At last, he settled on *Atatürk*, which means Father Turk, reflecting his view of himself as the Father of all Turks. He also decided that his first name, Mustafa, was too Arabic. From that point on, he would be known as Kemal Atatürk.

THE STORM CLOUDS OF WAR

While Turkish society was being reshaped in radical ways, the signs of international trouble were sweeping across Europe. First came the Italian invasion of Ethiopia in October 1935, after which Turkey joined the League of Nations sanctions, motivated at least in part by the evidence that Italy was moving troops into the Dodacanese Islands off the coast of Turkey. Next came Hitler's reoccupation of the Rhineland in March 1936. Following a meeting with the nations that had signed the Treaty of Lausanne (apart, of course, from Italy), Turkey was granted the right to reintroduce troops into the straits and police the waterways to ensure that commercial ships could pass through safely. As the world braced for war, Turkey was aligning itself with Britain, its old enemy.

As the international scene grew more troubled, Atatürk's health grew poor. He had been a frequent and intense drinker, and, as he reached the age of 53, his habits of long days spent working and long nights spent partying caught up with him. He began to suffer from cirrhosis of the liver caused by excessive drinking. But it was difficult for this active man to follow his doctors' orders to spend several months resting. On May 19, 1938, he celebrated the anniversary of his arrival at Samsun to launch the War of Independence with a parade through the capital, followed by a train trip south, where Turkey was gathering troops to patrol the border with Syria. The trip exhausted him, and would prove to be his last significant public appearance.

Experiencing liver failure and great discomfort, he agreed at last to his doctors' orders and moved to the yacht

Thermal Baths, Yalova, 1936

Turkey's natural hot springs have been renowned since antiquity. At Yalova, an important thermal resort on the southern shore of the Sea of Mamara, waters emerge from the ground heated at approximately 150 degrees Fahrenheit. These hot springs have been in continuous use since Roman times and are known for their therapeutic qualities, especially in treating rheumatic diseases.

that had been presented to him by the Turkish people. He was kept informed of political affairs and government activities as the yacht lay anchored near Istanbul, but for the most part he rested and tried to recover from the difficult illness. He would not succeed.

On October 16, 1938, Atatürk slipped into a coma. His family gathered around his bed, and political friends rushed from Ankara to Istanbul. Instructions were given as to the procedures that would be followed after his death—specifically, there would be no special religious services in mosques or mass gatherings. The constitution would prevail, the government would continue, and a new president would be chosen by the assembly.

But just as the instructions seemed to indicate that death

was imminent, Atatürk emerged from his coma. The assembly members returned to Ankara, and plans were made for Atatürk's appearance at the Republic Day celebration on October 29. But again, he fell ill, and could only listen to the bands marching past his yacht and the noise of the fireworks from his bed.

On November 8, Atatürk spoke his final words before slipping into a final coma. To his doctor he said, "Peace to you," which is the traditional Muslim reply to a greeting. Two days later, he died.

For seven days, mourners filed past their leader's body as it lay in state at Dolmabahce palace. Just as he had dictated, the republic and the government continued on. A new president was elected—Ismet Inönü, who had served as Prime Minister for many years before falling briefly out of favor with the president. He was the only candidate, and he was elected unanimously.

The mourning for Atatürk was real and heartfelt. For the people of Turkey, his death represented an end to an era of incredible transformation, an age that had seen their world changed. He had given them first a sense of national pride, and then a nation worthy of it. He had given them the power to become the masters of their own fate, no longer ruled by a monarch but instead governed by representatives they chose themselves. He had given them a new language and a new identity. Unlike many Muslim revolutionaries that would follow him in the Middle East, he resisted the temptation to create a military dictatorship based on violence and repression. Instead, he built a system of government designed to outlast one man. He built a society whose values were based on economic progress, rather than military victory.

Without Atatürk, a modern Turkey might never have existed. And now, his people would have to discover whether a modern Turkey could exist without him.

Mustafa Kemal Atatürk c. 1934

Shown in a file photograph from 1934, Atatürk was and is revered by Turks for his military and diplomatic victories that established Turkey as a republic.

5

Turkey After Atatürk

The republic Atatürk had shaped was strong, designed to outlast a single man's life. There was a system in place to ensure an orderly transfer of leadership, and the newly elected president was an experienced official. Inönü shared his predecessor's belief in the need to shape Turkey into a modern country, rooted in strong government rather than restrictive religious beliefs. Many of the policies that had begun under Atatürk were furthered after his death. The constitution was rewritten in Turkish. The effort to expand educational opportunities beyond the cities and into the countryside was aided by the creation of Village Institutes, where rural farmers and peasants were trained to serve as schoolteachers. State ballet and opera companies were formed to ensure that the Turkish people could enjoy the finest Western culture.

As fascist regimes in Germany, Italy, and Japan shouted against the evils of modern society, seeking to pull their countries back to an earlier, idealized past, Inönü continued to lead Turkey forward. As the world began to split into two sides in preparation for another war, the Turkish people were fortunate to have the diplomatically skillful Inönü as their leader. His experience, derived from years serving as Atatürk's prime minister, guaranteed him a certain measure of respect from the world leaders with whom he met. He negotiated alliances with France and Britain and simultaneously signed a non-aggression treaty with Germany. It was an astute move. Popular support lay with the Allies, but most politicians believed, at the war's beginning, that the Axis countries would win, particularly when, in 1941, German victories in the Balkans brought the German army to within 100 miles of Istanbul.

It was only toward the end of the war, when the Allies seemed certain of victory, that Turkey firmly abandoned its policy of neutrality and came out on the side of the Allies. In this way, Turkey was able to avoid the devastating kind of war that had crippled its economy and ripped its land apart at the beginning of the 20th century. It also permitted the republic to join the United Nations.

Many Turkish businessmen profited during the war due to the opportunities for foreign trade. There was no formal system of taxation, and as the government struggled to meet its expenses, a decision was made to collect revenue through an emergency tax. It went into effect on November 12, 1942, and created almost immediate chaos.

Those who had benefited the most from the wartime

economy were the farmers, who were mainly Muslim Turks, and the Istanbul business community, consisting mainly of Greeks, Jews, and Armenians. It quickly became clear that the tax was completely biased, both in amount and in enforcement. Businesses were to be taxed at a rate of between 50 and 75 percent. Large farm owners would not be required to pay more than five percent. For the vast majority of taxpayers, it was left to local tax boards to determine how much each individual should pay, without gathering any basic information such as how much that person earned or what amount of savings they had. The decisions were all final, and payment was due within 15 days. Taxpayers were classified based on their religion and nationality, with non-Muslims paying much more than Muslim citizens. After a month, the names of those who had not paid their taxes, as well as the amount they owed, was published, and shortly thereafter they were deported to labor camps. The vast majority of those arrested and sent to the labor camps were, not surprisingly, Greeks, Jews, and Armenians.

This policy enjoyed great support from the same sources that stood firmly behind Germany in the war, and it was not until Allied victory seemed certain, and Allied leadership spoke out critically against this clear example of intolerance, that the punished were gradually brought back from the labor camps. It was a sad moment for the republic. Foreign citizens were unjustly taxed and clearly suffered discrimination; the situation was not corrected until foreign pressure forced it to be.

THE POST-WAR WORLD

After the war had ended, Turkey enjoyed new and stronger relationships with the United States and Britain.

Both countries were concerned about the Russian leader Stalin and his plans to expand the Communist regime. They needed Turkey as a buffer, a country that would resist the Soviet influence.

Links with the democratic governments in Washington and London sparked public interest in moving away from the single-party system that had marked their government for many years. The Republican People's Party had shaped its country. Now, the Turkish people were interested in expanding the types of political representation available to them. In addition, Turkey's role in the newly formed United Nations was exposing it to discussions centering on the importance of democratically elected governments and the need for more than one party to ensure fair and representative government.

A group of disenchanted Republican People's Party members, desiring greater change than their party and its leaders offered, decided to leave their party and form a new one: the Democrat Party. Many of their fellow politicians viewed them as traitors, and at first it seemed quite possible that their efforts would be stamped out, using force if necessary. But Inönü, showing wisdom and restraint, instead recommended that Turkey, to avoid becoming a dictatorship, should permit the formation of an opposition party. Only two types of political parties were banned: Communist and religious.

The post-war Turkey was marked by greater numbers of citizens moving into urban areas. More citizens were educated. They read the newspaper, and kept informed of political news. It was a time of greater communication, as more households had telephones and listened to the radio. It was a time of greater mobility, as the public system of roads and railways expanded and improved. The Turkey Atatürk had dreamed of, a

Celal Bayar c. 1950

The new President of the Turkish Republic, Celal Bayar, and the members of the new Adnan Menderes cabinet are shown together following ceremonies in the National Assembly at Ankara on May 22, 1950.

literate, educated, cultured, and well-traveled society, was becoming a reality.

On May 14, 1950, Turkey held its first free and open elections. The Democrats, appealing to a desire for change, and with firm support from certain groups who were distinctly opposed to the People's Party (such as religious leaders, wealthy landowners, and a newly created middle class), won a majority of the seats in the Assembly, and Inönü was forced to resign. It is yet another tribute to the strong government set in place in Turkey that, after 27 years in power, the leadership was able to change hands without violence.

Although the party Atatürk had founded would never again win a majority of seats in the Assembly, his memory was far from dimmed following the election. The new president, Celal Bayar, a banker, had also served as prime minister under Atatürk from 1937 to 1939, and one of his first acts as president was to place the picture of the Father of Turks on Turkish stamps and money. But the new government was less strict in its regulation of the role of Islam. The principles of democracy from which the ruling party had taken its inspiration required freedom of expression, and gradually religious leaders, who had kept silent and been restricted during the years of Atatürk, were able to once again openly declare the need for a return to Islamic values and traditions. Mosques were rebuilt throughout Turkey, and Bayar's government reversed the policy of requiring the Islamic call to prayer to be made in Turkish. Instead, the faithful were once more called to worship in the traditional Arabic.

Religious education was restored in the public schools. It began in early 1949, when parents were given the opportunity to enroll their children in religious classes for two hours on Saturday afternoon. Many did. Little more than a year later, religious education had become mandatory in fourth and fifth grade. Where a short time before the Islamic classes were only offered if parents specifically requested them for their children, now parents were forced to specifically request that their children not be enrolled in the classes.

For four years, the Democratic Party was successful in its policies, and Turkey enjoyed a period of economic prosperity. Democratic plans for growth relied on less government intervention in industry and a greater focus on agriculture, by boosting the resources available to farmers and by increasing the number of tractors imported to expand the amount of land that could be cultivated and, in this way, increase production. In the beginning, these plans worked well. But as the economy slowed, and public dissatisfaction with the new policies increased, the Democratic Party became less "democratic" in its system of government. Worried about challenges from other parties, the Democrats took over the Republican People Party's newspaper and seized its property. By February 1954, the Democrats had passed a new censorship law, stating that anyone who published "inaccurate" information about the government (in other words, anything that was thought to be harmful to Turkey politically or economically) would be punished severely.

There were some within the Democrats who objected to these heavy-handed tactics, and many of them left to form their own separate but short-lived party, known as the Freedom Party. Elections in 1958 gave the Democrats a victory, but many questioned the results and felt that the votes had been incorrectly reported or somehow rigged. Matters came to a head in February 1960. The Republican People's Party had organized a meeting where the former president İnönü was scheduled to speak. The police were sent in to break up the meeting, causing great outrage among members of the opposition party. Two months later, the Democratic Party in the Assembly voted to create a commission whose duties would be to investigate members of the Republican People's Party and other opposition groups. The commission would be allowed to search property and people, and to arrest anyone deemed to be a threat to the state.

This clear attempt to eliminate anyone who might threaten the current group in power was too much for outraged Turkish citizens. Students formed protest groups in Istanbul and Ankara. The government retaliated by declaring martial law in those two cities. This calling in of the military to quiet rebellion in the streets of Turkey's two largest cities would prove to be a costly mistake for the leadership. The army quickly decided that the Democrats had gone too far. Early in the morning of May 27, 1960, General Cemal Gürsel led a team to arrest the politically powerful Democratic prime minister, Adnan Menderes, and the members of his government. The military had overthrown the government.

THE MILITARY RULES

As their first act, General Gürsel and 37 of the officers who had led the takeover announced that they would become the National Unity Committee, transferring the powers that had previously belonged to the Assembly to themselves. In the new government, Gürsel declared that he would serve as Prime Minister (a position that had, in recent years, become more powerful than the presidency), as well as Head of State and Minister of Defense. The leaders of the Democratic Party were charged with various crimes, including corruption and violating the constitution. Following a quick trial, Menderes and two other officials were executed, while other party members were imprisoned.

While the National Unity Committee had no immediate interest in sharing power, it did take steps to eliminate, in future, a concentration of too much power in a single political party. A new constitution was created, stating that Turkey would now have a Senate as well as its Assembly (the House of Representatives), and there

General Cemal Gürsel c. 1961

Early in the morning of May 27, 1960, General Cemal Gürsel led a team to arrest the powerful prime minister, Adnan Menderes, and the members of his government in a military overthrow.

would be a new Supreme or Constitutional Court charged with approving laws passed by the Senate and Assembly. The new constitution also granted the right to form unions, as well as mandating a system for universal medical care and social security.

After setting up systems to protect the rights of opposition parties, the military decided to step down in favor of a civilian government. General elections were held in 1961, but no single party won a majority of the seats. General Gürsel was elected as president. A coalition formed between the Republican People's Party and the newly formed Justice Party brought Inönü back as a political player, but only briefly. By 1965, the young Justice Party had gained in strength and numbers and won a majority of the votes, electing its young leader Süleyman Demirel to the position of prime minister.

The military believed so strongly in the ideals of Atatürk that their interventions in government continued for the next several decades. Each time that they saw the country straying from what they believed were the core beliefs of the constitution, or being overly influenced by politicians who placed their own needs over that of their country, they stepped in. In March 1971 they forced a change in government. In September 1980 they seized control of the country themselves. In June 1998 they forced a change in yet another government. And yet, the stability that the country had enjoyed under Atatürk would never again be completely replicated.

MORE PARTIES, MORE CONFUSION

The policies that the military had installed to prevent a single group from seizing power sparked the

development of a multitude of smaller parties appealing to more specialized interests. The development of
trade unions, coupled with an increasing number of
people moving to cities, encouraged more left-leaning
political groups to form, including the Confederation
of Reformists Workers' Unions (whose supporters
came mostly from trade union members), Dev Cenç
(a youth movement calling for revolution), the Workers'
Party of Turkey (a socialist group), and even the Turkish
Peoples' Liberation Army (an armed guerrilla movement). Meanwhile, the Democrats were released from
prison and by 1969 they were once more allowed to
form a party and solicit members. On the right, groups
that had split off from the Republican Peoples' Party
included the National Action Party and the National
Order Party (both groups calling for a return to Islamic
values and a renewed focus on Turkish nationalism).

While this wide array of choices for voters meant
that many different groups had a voice in politics, it
also meant that it was nearly impossible for any single
group to muster enough political support to accomplish
significant policies. Many of these parties were armed
and favored violent means to settle their differences.
Uprisings in Kurdistan increased the perception that the
government had lost control. On March 12, 1971, the
commanders of the three military branches announced
that they would step in to ensure the formation of a
strong and credible government intended to follow in
the tradition of Atatürk by creating reforms that
followed the spirit of the constitution. Demirel was
forced to resign. For the next 30 months, Turkey
would be governed by a series of governments that
essentially were put in place by and followed the direc-
tions of the military. Their main task was to restore
law and order and, in 11 of Turkey's 67 provinces,

martial law was declared to accomplish this. Anyone suspected of revolutionary activities against the government (including those guilty only of speaking out against the military takeover) were arrested. While the military-supported government talked loudly about its principles of freedom and democracy, its actions showed quite another side.

By the spring of 1973, the military reached a difficult crossroads. Their support within the weakened government was dwindling. They had two choices: either take over the government completely, removing any non-military people from power, or allow free elections to be held. They chose the second option, and elections were held in October 1973. The army's candidate for the presidency was defeated, and for the next seven years, political power shifted wildly between a series of small parties and weak governments. Political violence rose dramatically as extremist groups tried to seize power through aggressive tactics. As the government changed hands swiftly, averaging a new government every two years, corruption rose and public confidence in all politicians sank.

For a third time, the military stepped in. Early in the morning of September 12, 1980, General Kenan Evren overthrew the government, arrested the leaders of all major parties and set himself and five officers up as the National Security Council, intended to be a temporary military government The parliament, all political parties and even the unions were dissolved. Martial law was put into effect throughout Turkey. The public largely supported these actions to restore order and bring an end to the chaos.

One of the principal goals of the military regime was to eliminate the violence that had become a hallmark of the political process. Terrorists were hunted and arrested.

Coup of September 12, 1980

Early in the morning of September 12, 1980, General Kenan Evren overthrew the government, arrested the leaders of all the major parties, and set himself and five officers up as a temporary military government to restore order.

Concern about the spread of a more violent and revolutionary form of Islam (inspired by the Islamic revolution that overthrew the government in nearby Iran) sparked the government to crack down on all extremists. Guerrilla warfare was becoming a serious problem amongst the Kurdish population.

The military needed to correct, officially, some of the mistakes of the past. In 1982, a new constitution was drafted and approved that changed the system of government in Turkey. The new constitution created a more powerful president, who would be elected for a seven-year term. The president was given the power to appoint the prime minister and dismiss parliament. The parliament was reduced from two groups (the Assembly and the Senate) to a single representative body. The constitution also eliminated the influence of smaller bodies by dictating that no party receiving less than 10 percent of the votes would win a seat in parliament.

Under the new constitution, elections were called for in 1983. The military had hoped that the two parties it supported (the National Democratic Party and the Populist Party) would win handily, but instead it was the Motherland Party that won a majority of seats in the parliament. The Motherland Party had formed a coalition of liberal, nationalist, and Islamic groups, appealing to those disenchanted with the military's strong-arm tactics. But, more importantly for Turks discouraged by inflation and economic troubles, the Motherland Party was led by the well-known economist Turgut Özal.

Özal's prescription for economic healing included less dependence on government controls and greater foreign trade. From 1983 to 1987, as the Motherland Party ruled Turkey, these policies were quite successful. Neighboring Iran and Iraq were at war, and oil prices fell. The opportunities for trade were strong, and Turkey's economy grew rapidly. But the period of prosperity was to be short-lived. A recession crippled world economies in the late 1980s, and Turkey felt its effects too. Unemployment and inflation hit the country hard.

As Özal's government struggled to deal with economic troubles, it found itself facing an even more serious problem in its southeastern provinces. The violent outbursts from the Kurds had grown in intensity and frequency. Now they were fighting a war—a war for independence—within Turkey's own borders.

Two chiefs of the Kurdish army group c. 1925

6

The
Kurds

The Kurdish population has for many years sparked fierce debate, both within and outside Turkish borders, about exactly what constitutes a nation and what qualifies a people for their own territory. The Kurds, more than any other people, were left behind in the scattered ashes of the Ottoman Empire. Living principally in the region where Turkey, Iran, and Iraq come together, they are divided artificially, by borders and territorial claims, into three separate countries when in reality they are a single people unified by tribal customs. For many years they had sought independence from the nations that governed them, and yet no nation was willing to grant them this right.

For Turkey, the Kurdistan region was economically valuable

and not something to simply be handed away. Kurdistan was an important agricultural center, principally for its production of cotton and tobacco. Kurdistan also contained valuable oil and water resources. But the region was wracked by poverty. The great gains Atatürk and his successors had overseen in modernizing Turkey were not in evidence here.

In order to understand how strongly the Turkish government resisted the calls for independence from the Kurds, it is important to remember how bitterly the wars for independence were fought to ensure that no more of Turkey slipped away. All successors have held fast to this principle—that the territory of Turkey was defined in 1919 and none of it should be given up without a fight.

The Kurdish calls for independence were certainly not a new development. They dated back almost to the founding of modern Turkey. The policies that Atatürk had passed quite early on were deeply divisive in Kurdistan. The nation the Kurds wanted was a Muslim state, and so the decision to abolish the caliphate was alarming to them. More disturbing still were the later steps that would be taken to strengthen Turkey's national identity, but which in effect would erase more and more of the Kurdish identity. Places were no longer known by their Kurdish names, but only by Turkish ones. Turks moved in to Kurdistan to fill the middle- and senior-level government positions. Kurdish could no longer be spoken in courts or used in schools—laws that drastically affected the quality of education and legal representation available to the Kurdish people.

The result was an inevitable revolt among the people in 1925, as the effects of these nationalist policies became clear. Martial law was declared in all of Kurdistan and hundreds of rebels and suspected rebels were executed. But the most brutal actions were yet to come. Many of the Kurds were

Ishak Pasha's Palace, Dogubayazit (Bey Azit) c. 1931

Ishak Pasha's palace is a grand 18th-century 366-room Ottoman palace and fortress situated on a desolate Anatolian plain. Mount Ararat is in the far distant background. Construction was so detailed and laborious that it took 99 years to complete (1784). The gate's original gold-plated doors, master-pieces of Kurdish workmanship, were removed by Russian troops at the beginning of the 20th century. They are on display at St. Petersburg's Hermitage Museum in Russia.

Today, the Turkish government is attempting to restore the palace, but the continued conflict with the Kurds is affecting progress.

forcibly evacuated to western Anatolia. Villages were burnt, and the inhabitants—men, women and children— were killed. Cattle and animals were seized and removed, effectively condemning the people to starve to death. All religious groups were shut down.

Kurdish Village, Eastern Turkey, 1912

The Kurds—thought to number about 15 million today—live in contiguous areas of Iran, Iraq, and Turkey, a region generally referred to as Kurdistan although only Iran recognizes an area with that name.

Traditional Kurdish life was nomadic, revolving around the raising of goats and sheep. However, the enforcement of national boundaries after World War I (1914-18) forced most Kurds to settle in villages.

This brutal policing of their own people became a routine assignment for the Turkish army. In fact, the majority of Turkish military activities in the last 50 years, with few exceptions, have not been against aggressive invaders or foreign armies, but rather against the Kurds.

The rebellions continued to spring up as the Kurds

fought fiercely, both in Turkey and in neighboring regions, for their survival. By June 1934, Turkey had passed a strict law intended to stamp out the Kurdish rebellion for good. The law essentially divided Turkey into three regions: (1) regions reserved for people who already possessed the necessary "Turkish culture"; (2) regions where people of "non-Turkish culture" were to be moved in order to be successfully educated in Turkish language and culture; (3) regions that were to be evacuated. It is clear that the goal of this law was to eliminate any significant Kurdish population from any region, but the reality of trying to relocate three million people and spread them throughout the rest of Turkey prevented this law from being fully carried out.

The Republican People's Party, first under Atatürk and later his successors, carried out an effective campaign to quiet any rebellion—from Kurdistan in the southeast or anywhere. But the opening up of political power to other parties revived the cries for independence that had been silenced for many years. As the Democratic Party won power and restored a religious presence to the state, mosques and places of worship once more began to issue the call for a return to the traditional Islamic values that had flourished under the Ottomans.

The Kurds first rallied behind the Democrats, but soon became disillusioned when the reality of their policies differed greatly from what had been promised. However, politics had awakened the Kurdish people, and their homeland became an important campaign site for the many different parties that swept through Turkey, including a secret (because it was illegal) Kurdish party. The region was poor; increased mechanization and changes in farming had left many without jobs. They were undereducated, and living closely together. More significantly, while the rest of Turkey's population was

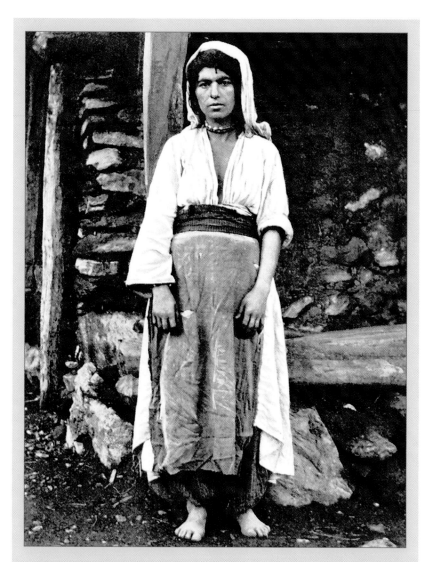

Kurdish Woman, Eastern Turkey, 1894

Under Atatürk's rule (1923-38), the Turkish Kurds were deprived of their national identity. Their official designation became "Mountain Turks" and their language was classified as a Turkish dialect. Kurds were forbidden to wear their distinctive costume.

Kurdish nationalism only intensified. As recently as 1996, the European Tariff Union delayed Turkey's entry because of its continued harsh treatment of the Kurds. Members of human rights groups publicized the atrocities—the destruction of Kurdish towns by Turkish military forces and the persecution of Kurdish leaders.

holding fairly steady, the population in Kurdistan was nearly doubling.

THE PKK

These were the conditions that concerned the Özal government in the 1980s, when news of increasing numbers of rebellions in Kurdistan reached Ankara. By the early 1980s, the violence was so widespread that two thirds of the Turkish army was patrolling Kurdistan, simply to keep the peace there. At first, it seemed that the violence was being contained. But then, in August 1984, a new series of attacks began against Turkish forces. The source was the Kurdistan Workers' Party (PKK).

This group was unusual among Turkish political parties because members were drawn largely from the working class. The PKK fought not merely for Kurdish rights, but also for workers rights. It was rebelling against the horrible conditions the average Turkish man or woman lived in, while wealthy merchants and the ruling Turkish government enjoyed prosperity and the benefits of wealth in far-distant Ankara and Istanbul. It was not merely a civil war, but also a class war, that the PKK was intent on launching. And their targets were not merely soldiers. In addition to attacking military bases and ambushing troops, the PKK also began killing wealthy landowners.

The government drastically increased the number of soldiers sent to patrol Kurdistan. By 1987, a state of emergency was declared in eight Kurdish provinces and a governor-general was appointed to coordinate the efforts of the various forces fighting the PKK. The governor-general was given wide-ranging powers, including the ability to evacuate villages if he felt it was necessary. Torture and physical abuse were common, and

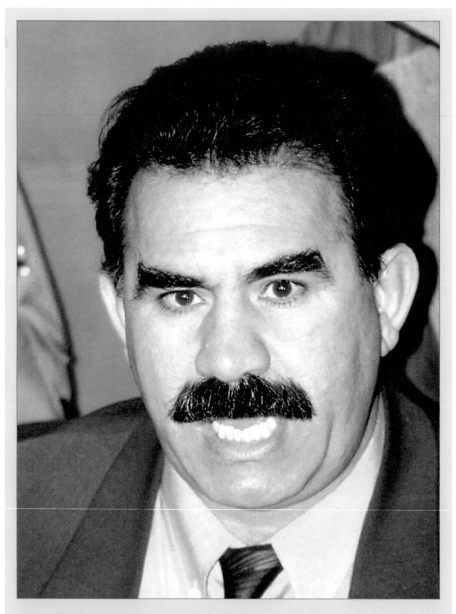

Abdullah Ocalan (Undated portrait)

Leader of the outlawed Kurdish rebel group, the PKK, or Kurdistan Workers' party. This group fought not only for Kurdish rights, but also for the rights of all workers. The group claimed responsibility for the assassination of Swedish Premier Olaf Palme in 1986, in retaliation for his agreement to extradite eight PKK rebels.

hundreds of villagers were routinely arrested and beaten until they confessed to aiding the PKK efforts.

These efforts backfired horribly. The majority of Kurdish villagers had not initially supported the PKK's campaign of intimidation and its arbitrary murder of landlords and village guards. But the brutal and violent methods of the government eclipsed those used by the PKK, and resulted in Kurdish families living in constant fear of imprisonment and abuse at the hands of the government. The number of Kurds supporting the PKK increased steadily.

In an effort to stamp out the PKK's newfound success in recruiting more support, President Özal announced that any Turkish publishing house that "falsely reflected events in the region" would be closed down. The same law gave the governor-general of Kurdistan the right to relocate anyone he thought needed to be moved out of the region to an area determined by the government. Hundreds of villages were burned following the passing of this law, and thousands left homeless.

The outrage of the Turkish people now joined the protests of the Kurdish population. The images of their own countrymen turned into refugees by the Turkish military was repugnant to the average person, and the government soon realized that the crisis had gone from a regional to a national one.

By 1992, President Özal had made a drastic change in his approach to the crisis, and was calling for recognition of the PKK as a possible participant in Turkey's political system. The PKK responded with a brief cease-fire in March of 1993, but the overtures for peaceful compromise made by President Özal vanished when he died on April 17, 1993. The new President, Sulayman Demirel, was less willing to negotiate with the PKK, and allowed the army to capitalize on the ceasefire by rounding up as many PKK fighters as it could find. In six weeks, the army killed about 100 people (fighters and civilians), arrested hundreds more, and resumed their destruction of homes and whole villages. The chance for peace had vanished. Ocalan announced that the ceasefire had ended.

A WIDENING CONFLICT

Under President Demirel, Turkey's first woman prime minister—Tansu Ciller—had been appointed, but she was unable or unwilling to challenge the military officers. The violence and intensity of the response grew at a frightening pace. Towns were subjected to military assaults. Civilians died in equal numbers to the soldiers and guerrilla fighters. The recently formed Kurdish political party, the HEP, was banned in July 1993.

The PKK responded by bringing the conflict to other parts of Turkey. Tourist sites in southern Turkey were attacked. European tourists in Kurdistan were seized as hostages. Turkish embassies and business locations in Europe were targeted and attacked. By the end of 1993, it was reported that 10,000 people had died since the conflicts first began in 1984. Within one year, that number would double.

The national nightmare was rapidly becoming a foreign policy disaster. As Turkey sought to establish itself as an active and democratic participant in the international community, these human rights abuses against its own people made investors and diplomats wary. The brutality of the military raised questions about the true nature of the Turkish government. And as more Kurds were heard calling for autonomy, or the right to govern their own region, rather than complete independence and separation from Turkey, the horrific response of the Turkish government

Suicide Bombing in the City of Van c. 1998

A woman from the PKK threw herself in front of a military bus and ignited bombs strapped to her waist in Van, Turkey on December 24, 1998. The girl, a teenage boy, and a passerby were killed—22 others were wounded. Such suicide bombings appear to have increased after Abdullah Ocalan was detained in Italy on November 12, 1998.

was increasingly difficult to understand or excuse.

The dreams of Atatürk for Turkey—a strong nation, unified by language, education, and Westernized ideas— seemed noble on the surface, but they have left an expensive legacy. The 12 million Kurds living in Turkey continue to pay the price.

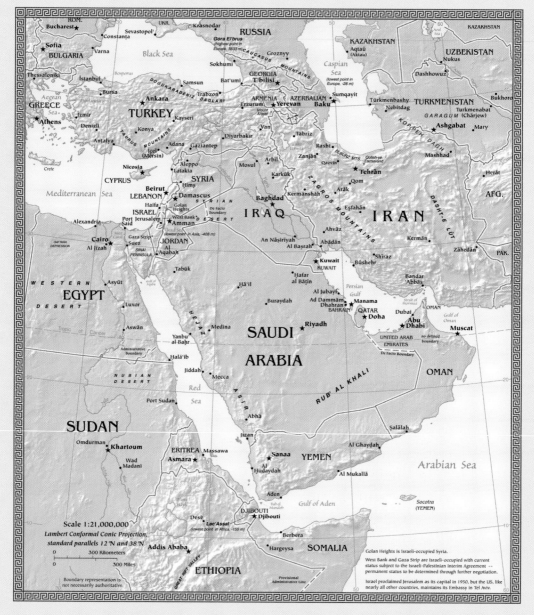

A Modern Map showing Turkey relative to the Middle East and Central Asia c. 2002.

7

Modern Turkey

For much of the early part of the 20th century, Turkey remained true to its early plans of building a Westernized society in matters of foreign policy. Turkey joined NATO in 1952, and applied to join the European Economic Community in 1959. It has, for many years, sought membership in the European Union, but this has been the subject of great debate, both within the European Union (from critics of Turkey's actions against the Kurds) and within Turkey itself (from the pro-Islamic militants who preach the need to turn away from the West).

Many of the difficulties Turkey currently faces in matters of foreign policy stem from actions taken against Cyprus. Cyprus is a large island located in the eastern part of the Mediterranean Sea (the third largest island in the Sea, after Sicily and Sardinia). It is found about 40 miles south of Turkey. It was one of the few territories from the Ottoman Empire that remained a British colony well after the rest of the empire had been carved up. But by the 1950s, the people of Cyprus were demanding what they felt was their long-overdue independence.

What should have been a simple, straightforward process—to grant independence or not—turned out to be anything but clear. Not only Britain, but also Greece and Turkey felt that they had a specific and strategic interest in Cyprus. The majority of the population of Cyprus is Greek-speaking, and traces of Greeks on Cyprus date back to the earliest points in recorded history. A frequent target of invaders because of its strategic position, Cyprus was conquered by Ottoman Turks in the 1500s, and it remained a part of the Ottoman Empire until 1878, when the island was leased to the British in exchange for British support against the Russian army. When the Ottoman Empire sided with Germany in World War I, the British seized control of Cyprus, and in 1925 they proclaimed it a British colony.

The Turks, Greeks, and British all managed to live in relatively peaceful coexistence until demands for independence became more frequent and were, each time, denied by the British. Greece soon supported the call for independence, feeling that as the majority of the population was Greek, an independent Cyprus would, essentially, become an extension of Greece. Turkey objected, saying that the island's proximity to Turkey posed a strategic threat. The Turkish position was that Cyprus should either remain British or be divided into separate Turkish and Greek regions.

The debate caused tension within NATO and the United Nations, as the international community was faced with the uneasy prospect of choosing sides between two members of those organizations. Ultimately, following a series of diplomatic negotiations, it was announced on August 16, 1960, that Cyprus would be an independent state, although essentially the independence was quite limited. Britain was given the right to maintain two military bases in the southern and eastern regions of the island. Greece and Turkey were also given the right to maintain small military units on the island, and to oversee their respective communities. The system of government was similarly restricted. The president would always be Greek; the vice-president Turkish. Each community would be judged by its own separate courts; legal matters involving both communities would be judged in a trial presided over by two judges.

This awkward arrangement served only to further divide the people living on Cyprus. Tensions rose steadily until July 1974, when the Greek president was overthrown in a coup. The leaders of the new Greek government proclaimed that Cyprus must be united with Greece. Turkey responded quickly and with force. Early in the morning of July 20, Turkish forces began landing on the northern part of Cyprus, both by sea and from the air, as landing craft pulled up on the shores and paratroopers dropped into the Turkish communities. For several days, the Turkish troops pushed steadily inward, until they occupied nearly 40 percent of the island, sending thousands of Greek refugees into the remaining portions of Cyprus.

The prospect of Turkey and Greece going to war became increasingly real as the dispute widened to include arguments over territory in the Aegean Sea. Initial NATO response was tentative, designed to limit the crisis rather than decisively end it. But in the fall of 1974, the United States took the unexpected step of declaring an arms embargo against Turkey, freezing the delivery of $200 million in weapons. The embargo lasted

Turkish Troops Occupy Cyprus c. 1974

In July 1974 the Greek president was overthrown in a coup. The leaders of the new Greek government proclaimed that Cyprus must be united with Greece and Turkey responded by landing troops on the northern part of the island.

for several years, until U.S. president Jimmy Carter took decisive steps to end it. But the effects of the Cyprus situation, and the various countries' roles in it, are felt to this day.

For Turkey, the experience in Cyprus made it clear that a purely pro-Western diplomatic policy is inadequate. Turkey felt cheated at the response of its Western allies, particularly the United States, to the initially aggressive action of the Greeks, and angered at the arms embargo resulting from what it claimed was merely an action taken to protect the Turkish community on Cyprus. Turkey reached out to the Soviet Union, forming trade alliances with the nation it had once regarded as its greatest enemy. When the Soviet Union collapsed, the Turkish government formed agreements with many of its former states, including those in the Balkans and Central Asia.

While Greece has been admitted to the European Union, Turkey's repeated attempts to gain admission to this important organization have not yet been successful. For Turkey, the economic importance of Europe is clear—about 50 percent of Turkey's exports are destined for Europe and, in return, approximately 50 percent of its imports come from there. To the Turks, it is particularly disturbing that Cyprus was declared eligible for membership in 1993, and is in fact in line for membership ahead of Turkey.

The links with NATO have continued, despite frequent disagreements over strategic and diplomatic issues. In Bosnia, Turkey sided with the plight of the Muslim community and actively participated in UN and NATO actions in the region. Similarly, Turkey supported UN actions against Iraq in the Persian Gulf War, allowing UN and NATO troops access to its military bases. The decision proved an expensive one, as the subsequent embargo against Iraq would cost Turkey millions of dollars as the revenue from oil pipelines passing through Turkey disappeared.

THE ROLE OF ISLAM

The fate of the Kurds continues to haunt those shaping Turkey's domestic and international policy into the 21st century. Turkish military actions against the Kurds have sparked international criticism on human rights issues, and dominated debates about Turkey's possible role in the European Union.

The war has been costly not only in terms of prestige, but in terms of actual cash, as well. Turkey spends billions of dollars each year to fight the Kurds, and its foreign debt is soaring. Unemployment is high, and the modernization that shaped cities like Istanbul and Ankara is in little evidence in more rural areas.

As dissatisfaction with government policies spreads among the people, the conditions are ripe for revolt, and lurking constantly on the edge is the possibility of Islamic militant action. The government continues to waver between opening the door slightly to permit some religious freedom, and stamping out all Islamic activities and particularly political parties for fear that they should become too powerful and steer Turkey backward in time to the days of the caliph.

The fear of Islamic revival has dictated much of recent Turkish policy toward the activities of political parties. Since 1980, there has been a marked increase in visible displays of Islamic culture in Turkey—more Islamic books and prayer manuals are being published, more women are wearing headscarves, more mosques are being built, and religious classes are becoming increasingly popular.

In elections in December 1995, the political party that won the largest portion of the vote was the Islamic Welfare Party. A shift in thinking was occurring, as support for the traditional ideals and values represented by the Welfare Party came not only from rural areas but also from the cities. The Welfare Party urged stronger alliances with Middle Eastern nations and less reliance on Europe and the United States. It encouraged a greater role for Islam in public life. It failed to form a successful coalition, but its ability to garner support signaled an important shift in political thought. Most recently, the government has veered between allowing these parties a limited role in government and banning them outright, as was done in 2000 to the Welfare Party and in 2001 to the main opposition party, the pro-Islamic Virtue Party.

As Turkey struggles with economic problems, the stories of the glorious old days of the Ottoman Empire have awakened a longing for the time when Turkey was the center of the Muslim world. The Islamic movement focuses on the importance of an identity that overrules nationality or location—identity as a Muslim is more important that any other identity a person can have. The conflict with the goals Atatürk had for Turkey is clear. In the ideal Islam society, a greater community of believers is created that overrules national identity. At its extreme, Islam may come to represent a rejection of Western values and society. Turkey's geographic location—bridging the gap between Europe and Asia—is reflected in this conflict, as the nation swings back and forth between Western and Arabic culture.

A DREAM UNFULFILLED

As Turkey enters the 21st century, it remains a nation of contrasts. Its culture is marked in turn by both Arabic and Western influences. It struggles to shake off the dusty legacy of its Ottoman past, and then in turn embraces the important role it plays within the Islamic world. It clings to the dreams of Western democratic ideals first outlined by Atatürk, and yet fiercely fights the right of its Kurdish population to govern itself and eliminates political parties whose views and popularity seem to threaten the government. It supports the need for international partnerships, and yet turns away when its partners express concern about Turkey's human rights record.

Mausoleum of Mustafa Kemal Atatürk c. 1997

The resting place of Atatürk has become a pilgrimage site for those who see themselves as loyal to his principles of a modern Turkish republic.

Turkey is adjacent to so many potentially troublesome regions that its importance as an ally is clear. Its presence is a balance to the more militant regimes in Iran and Iraq. It is an important site for NATO actions to quiet the troubled regions of the former Yugoslavian republic. Its strict secular policy has helped to hold back the forces of more aggressive Islamic regimes. In many ways, Turkey has become the important Western ally that Atatürk had planned. And yet its policies in recent years have made it clear that Turkish policy is dictated by national, rather than international, concerns.

The dreams Atatürk had for this young nation have, in some ways, come true. The Republic of Turkey, the country that rose from the ashes of the Ottoman Empire, has become a nation with clear boundaries and a clear identity. Its people are Turks, they speak their own Turkish language, and they fiercely resist any attempt to redraw their borders or disperse their land.

And yet the very vision that freed Turkey from the shackles of domination by European powers has still left it imprisoned. The clear attempts to keep Turkey from returning to the days of rule by a caliph have left it uneasy with any strong expression of religion or of any clear role for Islamic parties in a national government. The inflexible attitude about what does and does not constitute Turkish territory brought it to the brink of war with Greece, alienated many of its allies in the wake of action in Cyprus, and is certainly responsible for the bloody civil war in Kurdistan.

Turkey is today a nation still shaping its identity. It is on the brink of economic growth, on the brink of political stability, on the brink of democracy. And yet, for now, something still holds it back. The dreams of Atatürk remain just that—dreams, haunting his people as they strive towards shaping them into reality.

The creation of the Republic of Turkey at the beginning of the 20th century was one of the most wondrous transformations in history. Turkey stands today as a testament to the legacy of Atatürk. But whether it will move beyond his legacy, or remain a prisoner of it, remains uncertain.

1881	Mustafa Kemal is born in Salonica.
1907	The C.U.P. is formed.
1908	Young Turk revolution is successful, and a new government is formed.
1909	C.U.P. military force marches on Istanbul after counter-revolution. A new sultan is proclaimed.
1914	World War I begins. Turkey enters war after forming alliance with Germany.
1915–16	Mustafa Kemal successfully repels attempted Allied invasion of Gallipoli.
1917	British forces capture Baghdad.
1919	Mustafa Kemal issues "Declaration of Independence" after landing at Samsun.
1920	San Remo Conference is held, and the Ottoman Empire is divided.
1921	Name of new state is declared to be Turkey.
1922	Monarchy is abolished in Turkey, and the sultan leaves.
1923	Treaty of Lausanne is signed. Assembly declares that Turkey is a republic. Mustafa Kemal is elected as its first president. Capital is moved from Istanbul to Ankara.
1924	All members of the Ottoman royal family are expelled from Turkey and caliphate is abolished. Religious courts and schools are banned.
1925	Turkey adopts the Gregorian (Western) calendar and bans the fez.
1928	Turkey is officially declared a secular (non-religious) republic. Arabic numbers and alphabet are abolished; Western alphabet and numbers are legally required.
1935	Law is passed requiring Turkish people to take a last name (surname).
1938	Atatürk dies.
1950	First free and open elections are held. Democratic Party wins.
1952	Turkey joins NATO.
1959	Turkey applies for membership in the European Economic Community.

1960 Military overthrows government for the first time.

1971 Military again overthrows government in an attempt to restore law and order.

1974 Kurdistan Workers Party (PKK) formed by Abdullah Ocalan. Turkey invades Cyprus.

1982 New constitution creates more powerful president, elected for a seven-year term.

1984 PKK launches a series of attacks against Turkish forces.

1993 Sulayman Demirel becomes president and appoints Turkey's first woman prime minister, Tansu Ciller.

2001 Main opposition party, pro-Islamic Virtue Party, is officially banned.

Further Reading

BOOKS:

Kinross, Lord. *Atatürk: The Rebirth of a Nation*. London: Weidenfeld and Nicolson, 1964.

Mango, Andrew. *Atatürk*. New York: The Overlook Press, 1999.

McDowall, David. *A Modern History of the Kurds*. New York: I.B. Tauris, 1996.

O'Ballance, Edgar. *The Kurdish Struggle*. New York: St. Martin's Press, Inc., 1996.

Sheehan, Sean. *Turkey*. New York: Marshall Cavendish, 1993.

ON THE WEB:

www.bbc.co.uk/history

www.britannica.com

www.discoveryschool.com

www.historychannel.com

www.schoolhistory.co.uk

www.un.org/pubs/cyberschoolbus/

Armstrong, H.C. *Grey Wolf*. London: Arthur Barker, Ltd., 1933.

Ciment, James. *The Kurds: State and Minority in Turkey, Iraq and Iran*. New York: Facts on File, 1996.

Couloumbis, Theodore A. *The United States, Greece and Turkey: The Troubled Triangle*. New York: Praeger Publishers, 1983.

Fromkin, David. *A Peace to End All Peace*. New York: Avon Books, 1989.

Garber, G.S. *Caravans to Oblivion: The Armenian Genocide, 1915*. New York: John Wiley and Sons, 1996.

Hale, William. *The Political and Economic Development of Modern Turkey*. New York: St. Martin's Press, 1981.

Jackh, Ernest. *The Rising Crescent: Turkey Yesterday, Today and Tomorrow*. New York: Farrar & Rinehart, Inc., 1994.

Kinross, Lord. *Atatürk: The Rebirth of a Nation*. London: Weidenfeld and Nicolson, 1964.

Kramer, Heinz. *A Changing Turkey*. Washington, D.C.: Brookings Institution Press, 2000.

Lewis, Bernard. *The Emergence of Modern Turkey*. New York: Oxford University Press, 1961.

Mango, Andrew. *Atatürk*. New York: The Overlook Press, 1999.

McDowall, David. *A Modern History of the Kurds*. New York: I.B. Tauris, 1996.

O'Ballance, Edgar. *The Kurdish Struggle: 1920-94*. New York: St. Martin's Press, Inc., 1996.

Rustow, Dankwart A. *Turkey: America's Forgotten Ally*. New York: Council on Foreign Relations, 1987.

Tapper, Richard (ed.). *Islam in Modern Turkey*. New York: I.B. Tauris, 1991.

WEB SITE SOURCES:

www.bbc.co.uk

www.britannica.com

www.discoveryschool.com

www.historychannel.com

www.un.org

Unless otherwise credited the photographs in this book are from the Royal Geographic Society Picture Library. Most are being published for the first time.

The Royal Geographic Society Picture Library provides an unrivaled source of over half a million images of the peoples and landscapes from around the globe. Photographs date from the 1840s onwards on a variety of subjects including the British Colonial Empire, deserts, exploration, indigenous peoples, landscapes, remote destinations, and travel.

Photography, beginning with the daguerreotype in 1839, is only marginally younger than the Society, which encouraged its explorers to use the new medium from its earliest days. From the remarkable mid-19th century black-and-white photographs to color transparencies of the late 20th century, the focus of the collection is not the generic stock shot but the portrayal of man's resilience, adaptability and mobility in remote parts of the world.

In organizing this project, we have incurred many debts of gratitude. Our first, though, is to the professional staff of the Picture Library for their generous assistance, especially to Joanna Wright, Picture Library Manager.

HEATHER LEHR WAGNER is an editor and writer. She has an M.A. in government from the College of William and Mary and a B.A. in political science from Duke University. She is also the author of *Iran, The Kurds,* and *Saudi Arabia* in the CREATION OF THE MODERN MIDDLE EAST series.

AKBAR S. AHMED holds the Ibn Khaldun Chair of Islamic Studies at the School of International Service of American University. He is actively involved in the study of global Islam and its impact on contemporary society. He is the author of many books on contemporary Islam, including *Discovering Islam: Making Sense of Muslim History and Society,* which was the basis for a six-part television program produced by the BBC called *Living Islam.* Ahmed has been visiting professor and the Stewart Fellow in the Humanities at Princeton University, as well as visiting professor at Harvard University and Cambridge University.